Perugia, Assisi & Southern Umbria

Julius Honnor

9/2245153

Credits

Footprint credits
Editor: Nicola Gibbs
Production and layout: Emma Bryers
Maps: Kevin Feeney
Cover: Pepi Bluck

Publisher: Patrick Dawson
Managing Editor: Felicity Laughton
Advertising: Elizabeth Taylor
Sales and marketing: Kirsty Holmes

Photography credits
Front cover: Khirman Vladimir/
Shutterstock.com
Back cover: Gkuna/Shutterstock.com

Printed in Great Britain by CPI Antony Rowe,
Chippenham, Wiltshire

MIX
Paper from
responsible sources
FSC® C013604
www.fsc.org

Every effort has been made to ensure that
the facts in this guidebook are accurate.
However, travellers should still obtain advice
from consulates, airlines, etc, about travel
and visa requirements before travelling.
The authors and publishers cannot accept
responsibility for any loss, injury or
inconvenience however caused.

Publishing information
Footprint *Focus Perugia, Assisi &
Southern Umbria*
1st edition
© Footprint Handbooks Ltd
May 2013

ISBN: 978 1 909268 11 1
CIP DATA: A catalogue record for this book
is available from the British Library

® Footprint Handbooks and the Footprint
mark are a registered trademark of
Footprint Handbooks Ltd

Published by Footprint
6 Riverside Court
Lower Bristol Road
Bath BA2 3DZ, UK
T +44 (0)1225 469141
F +44 (0)1225 469461
footprinttravelguides.com

Distributed in the USA by Globe Pequot
Press, Guilford, Connecticut

The content of Footprint *Focus Perugia,
Assisi & Southern Umbria* has been taken
directly from Footprint's *Umbria & Marche*
guide, which was researched and written
by Julius Honnor.

Contents

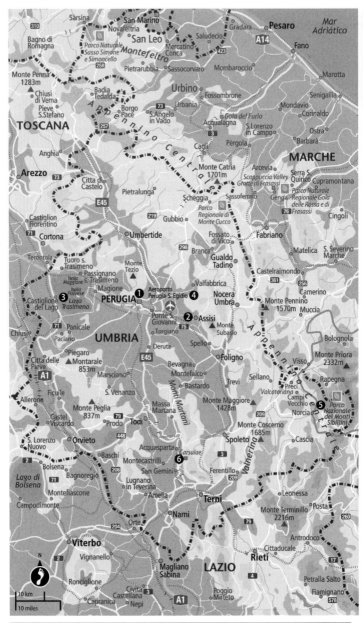

Umbria is Italy's only landlocked region, and this part of the country is dominated by its hills. The high Apennines are less a barrier than an identifying birthmark, a commonality of landscape and lifestyle.

Equidistant from Rome and Florence, Umbria has long been marked by the comings and goings to the north and south, but never swamped by them. Essentially rural, its hill towns are often exceptionally beautiful but are usually beacons of stone in a green, hilly, wooded world. And though the Etruscans and Romans dominate the museums, it is the medieval period that has left the deepest impression on the contemporary urban psyche, with many streets having changed little in 500 years.

Religion has made its mark here too, but even at its holiest it is a pastoral spirituality – not for nothing did St Francis go to live in the woods, preach to the birds and befriend the wolf.

The food and wine may not generally be complex but they are no less delicious for that. And the art and architecture is astounding but also approachable, largely because few of Tuscany's tour groups make it this far south or east.

But to characterize Umbria as 'Tuscany without the tourists', as many do, is to do it a disservice, for this is an area proud of its own nature. It is rustic but also creative and individual, seldom brash or ostentatious, and all the more wonderful for that.

Planning your trip

Places to visit in Perugia, Assisi and Southern Umbria

The green heart of Italy has hills aplenty – many topped with medieval towns – as well as mountains and lakes. The landscape is stunning, with enormous panoramic vistas around every corner. The spine of the region, the Apennine range – snow-capped in winter and then enrobed in spring flowers – makes ideal walking country. Or you could fling yourself off the top with help from a paraglider, or rush down whitewater rapids in a raft.

From ancient Rome to the Renaissance, from Raphael to Ravanelli, the wealth of historical and artistic treasures in places such as Assisi and Orvieto is extraordinary, while towns such as Perugia have lively universities to add youthful spice to the cultural mix.

Central Umbria

Perugia, the region's biggest city, and **Assisi**, its biggest tourist attraction, sit facing each other across the northern neck of the Valle Umbra, a large plain that was once under water. Still living a watery existence – just – is **Lago Trasimeno** to the west. Perugia and Assisi are very different places: the former a lively university town famed for its summer jazz festival and its chocolate; the latter one of the holiest places in Christendom, home of St Francis and St Clare, and the site of frescoes that changed the face of art.

Stray from the souvenir-laden main streets of Assisi, or the wide, paved thoroughfare of Perugia, and you will find yourself lost among a maze of narrow medieval lanes, with cats lying in the shade of ancient arches and women hanging washing from high windows. And Perugia's cultural life goes much deeper than its summer festivals: late into the night, when the rest of Umbria has long since gone to bed, music issues from chic wine bars and gritty student pubs.

Shallow Lake Trasimeno is a cool antidote to the two towns, with regular boats to its indolent islands and a beach life of sorts around its edges. And there are other escapes too – behind Assisi, **Monte Subasio** rises steeply, with good summer walking and cross-country skiing in winter.

Valle Umbra and southeast Umbria

South of Assisi, a series of steep hill towns presides over the flat plains below, each prettier than the last. **Spello**, **Trevi** and **Spoleto** all retain their strong medieval identities, while **Montefalco** adds the bonus of a successful wine industry. **Bevagna** is flatter, but no less lovely.

The striking town of **Norcia** was the birthplace of the twin saints Benedict and Scholastica, the first Western monk and nun. Beyond, further south and east, the landscape changes: the Apennines rise to some of their most spectacular heights in the **Parco Nazionale dei Monti Sibillini**, straddling Umbria and Marche, a mountainous land of wild boar, wolves and morning mists. Beech woods cling to folds in the hills while the enormous high plains are home to wild flowers and fields of lentils.

Southwest Umbria

The town of **Orvieto**, built on, and into, a huge layer cake of volcanic rock, is another of Umbria's centres, dominated by a gargantuan cathedral visible from afar. Decorated both inside and out with fascinating, if occasionally nightmarish, bas-relief and frescoes, it is one of the region's must-see buildings. Orvieto is a wine centre too – its crisp white is a good accompaniment to a meal in one of its excellent restaurants.

Nearby **Todi** is yet another hill town, with an excellent September arts festival and some huge Roman cisterns underneath its striking piazza. **Narni**, from which CS Lewis probably took the name for his fantasy land Narnia, is a little-visited town with a fascinating underground network. The geographic centre of Italy, it has remarkable Roman remains, which residents of pretty nearby **Amelia** see as rather modern – their town having been founded before Rome itself. To the north there is more of ancient Rome, in the shape of the abandoned town of **Carsulae**, whose romantic ruins occupy a bucolic spot among thickly wooded hills.

Best time to visit Perugia, Assisi and Southern Umbria

Winter in Umbria is cold with temperatures dropping close to freezing at night. Snowfall is common across the region, especially at higher altitudes, where cross-country skiing is popular. However, January is the second driest month and the weather is often crisp and sunny. **Carnevale** in February sees a week of feasting and processions in some places.

Spring can be slow in arriving, especially at higher altitudes where the snow lingers. Even at lower levels the temperature rarely hits 15°C. Easter is celebrated with plenty of pomp and ceremony. At night the temperature drops and there can still be frosts, but the days are becoming warmer.

As the snows melt, the mountains become covered in a carpet of wild flowers. Timing depends on the weather, but crocuses, blue squill, orchids and narcissi usually flower first, followed by geraniums, buttercups, peonies and tulips in June and then cornflowers, daisies and poppies. Butterflies also enjoy the show. At lower levels May is usually pleasantly warm with maximum temperatures averaging 22°C.

By June, the last remnants of snow in the high mountains melt away as the average maximum temperature climbs to 26°C and the region's many summer festivals get under way. In July the average maximum temperature is 29°C but can reach the mid-30s. However, nights are seldom oppressively warm and the hills offer a cool respite. The beaches become busy with italians and northern Europeans on their summer holidays and ice creams become an almost obligatory part of the evening *passeggiata*. Many towns host age-old celebrations, often with a medieval theme.

In August the inland towns empty as people head to the coast; you may have to fight to get a beach umbrella. Hot, sunny weather predominates, punctuated by occasional heavy thunderstorms. Many of the locals who stay behind are involved in traditional festivals, and improvised outdoor eateries spring up in the medieval hill towns as figs ripen and shops fill with delicious local tomatoes. On 15 August Italy comes to a complete standstill for **Ferragosto** (see page 17).

By autumn, the heat of summer tails off and there are mists in the mornings over the valleys, as Italians troop back to work. Nights are often cold and the first snows may fall on the peaks of the Sibillini. Grapes are havested and porcini mushroooms, gathered from the woods, become increasingly popular on restaurant menus.

November is usually the wettest month; the average temperature drops below 10°C for the first time but there can still be some pleasantly warm days. The first new olive oil pressings become available from the year's crop and are best consumed fresh.

Snow is possible in December though white Christmases are only likely at higher levels. On average the temperature falls to only 9°C but December is usually drier than November and somtimes seasonally crisp, frosty weather creates a festive mood. **Capodanno** (New Year) is welcomed with fireworks, feasting and lentil soup.

Getting to Perugia, Assisi and Southern Umbria

Air

From UK and Ireland   Flights to Milan or Rome depart from UK and Irish destinations frequently. Alternatively, fly right to the heart of Umbria with **Ryanair** ⓘ *www.ryanair.com*, which flies from London Stansted to Perugia three times a week in winter, five times a week in summer, and to Ancona, in neighbouring Marche, four times a week in winter and daily in summer. Other central Italian regional airports such as Bologna, Pisa and Rimini are also possible arrival points for travel to the region.

From North America   There are no direct flights to Umbria from North America; the closest connections are via Rome or Milan. **Continental**, **American Airlines** and **Delta** fly direct from New York to Rome Fiumicino and Milan. **Delta** also flies to both cities from Toronto via New York.

From rest of Europe   Airports in Rome and Milan are well connected to every major European city.

Airport information Perugia San Francesco d'Assisi ⓘ *T075-592141, www.airport. umbria.it*. Perugia airport has expanded in recent years but is still small enough that arriving and departing is generally a generally quick and easy process. The airport is on the plain about 20 minutes' drive from both Perugia and Assisi; a taxi costs about €30 to either. **Sulga** ⓘ *T800-099661, www.sulga.it*, buses meet Ryanair flights and go to piazza Italia in the centre of Perugia for €8 (€14 return). There are also **Umbria Mobilità** ⓘ *www. umbriamobilita.it*, services to Perugia and Assisi. Car rental companies at the airport include **Avis**, **Hertz** and **Maggiore** and there's a small information desk.

Rail

Rail journeys involve taking the **Eurostar** to Paris, then onwards overnight sleepers to the most convenient Italian rail hubs: Milan (five hours from Perugia), Rome (2½ hours) or Bologna (three hours). For international tickets and information, contact **Rail Europe** ⓘ *T0870-548 8848, www.raileurope.com*. For Italian train information search **Trenitalia**

① *T06-6847 5475, www.trenitalia.it*, and for Umbrian regional transport, **Umbria Mobilità** ① *www.umbriamobilita.it*. Rail travel to Perugia takes between 2½ and five hours (from Rome and Milan respectively). **Motorail** ① *www.autoslaaptrein.nl*, services run from the Netherlands to Livorno or Bologna, allowing you to drive on and drive off.

Road
Bus/coach Eurolines ① *T08717-818178, www.eurolines.co.uk*, operates services from London Victoria to Milan, changing in Paris and taking around 24 hours. Prices start at £62. From there, a **Sulga** ① *www.sulga.it*, coach service travels from Milan to Perugia's piazza Italia four times a week (seven hours). Sulga also runs numerous bus and coach services throughout Umbria and also several to Rome.

Car The 1050-km journey from London to Perugia will take around 18 hours' driving time. The A1 *autostrade* (motorway) that splices Italy vertically provides a fairly direct route to Perugia (a 4½-hour drive from Milan). Exit at Valdichiana, approximately 100 km after Florence, and follow signs for Perugia.

Transport in Perugia, Assisi and Southern Umbria

The major towns in the region are mostly connected by train. Train stations are often at the peripheries of towns, however, meaning that a bus journey or taxi ride is necessary to reach the town centre. Buses also run to most places, though they are often infrequent, and just about non-existent on Sundays. For the freedom to go to more out-of-the-way places, when you want, a car is invaluable, especially if you plan to stay in an *agriturismo* in the countryside.

Touring Club Italiano produces good general maps of the area – a free version of the Umbria half of their *Umbria e Marche* map is often available in tourist offices. For more detail, **Kompass** does a series of walking and cycling maps that cover some of the region's most popular areas. For real detail of local areas, maps produced by the **Club Alpino Italiano** are hard to beat, but equally hard to get hold of, though they can usually be found in towns on the edges of national and regional parks.

Rail
Two main lines serve the region: the **Rome to Ancona** line, via Spoleto and Foligno; and the **Rome to Florence** line up the Tiber Valley, via Orvieto. Fast Eurostar trains run along both of these routes, as well as ordinary (and cheaper) regional trains. There is also a branch from **Foligno to Terontola** via Perugia, Assisi and Spello, connecting both of the major Umbrian lines; some Eurostar trains use this route, though it's often necessary to change at Foligno or Terontola.

To complicate matters further, there is a private train line, now part of the **Umbria Mobilità network** ① *www.umbriamobilita.it*, running from Terni in the south via Todi and Perugia to Città di Castello in the north, and then on to Sansepolcro, in Tuscany. In Perugia this uses a different station – Sant'Anna – in addition to the mainline station.

Tickets are cheap, though the price is approximately double for the faster, more comfortable Eurostar trains; www.trenitalia.com has timetables and prices. Some examples of journey times and single, second-class fares are: Perugia to Assisi, 20 minutes, €2.40; Perugia to Spello, 30 minutes, €3; Perugia to Spoleto, one hour, €4.80.

Tickets (except for journeys on the regional Umbria Mobilità line) can be booked at www.trenitalia.com, where the type of train is indicated with the initials ES (Eurostar),

IC (Intercity) or REG (Regional). Amica fares are cheaper advance tickets (if you can find one), flexi fares costs more but are flexible, and standard fares are just that. In general, it's cheaper and more convenient to book online or at ticket machines for the journeys you need to take than it is to buy a pass. When using a service such as Eurostar Italia or InterCity, booking is advised and a surcharge in addition to a pass will often be required; passes therefore lose their thrift factor for tourists. On many Italian trains it's possible to travel 'ticketless', meaning you get on the train and quote your booking reference when the conductor comes round.

Booking and buying tickets at the counter or via machines in train stations is convenient if you can't access the internet. Remember, you must validate train tickets at the yellow stamping machines before boarding.

Road

Bicycle A mountain bike is a good way of seeing some of the region's countryside, but mostly the towns are too hilly and cobbled for bikes to be much use for getting around. Towns are also generally small enough for you to be able to walk anywhere fairly quickly. Outside of the towns, Italians are keen weekend lycra wearers, but it hasn't done anything to make cycling on the roads any safer. If you want to cycle for pleasure, Lake Trasimeno (see page 43) and Orvieto (see page 88) are good places.

Bus/coach **Sulga** ① *www.sulga.it*, runs buses between Perugia and Rome, Naples, Milan and Florence. **Sena** ① *www.sena.it*, is a low-cost bus service serving Siena, Milan and Perugia. **Spoletina** ① *www.spoletina.com*, covers Spoleto, Trevi, Montefalco and Spello. **Umbria Mobilità** ① *www.umbriamobilita.it*, runs services in Perugia and Assisi, as well as longer (*extraurbani*) services to Todi, Castiglione del Lago and Gubbio. Buses mainly run from outside, or at least near, train stations.

Car EU nationals taking their own car need to have an International Insurance Certificate (also known as a *Carte Verde*). Those holding a non-EU licence also need to take an International Driving Permit with them. Unleaded petrol is *benzina*, diesel is *gasolio*.

Italy has strict laws on drink driving: steer clear of alcohol to be safe. The use of mobile telephones while driving is illegal. Other nuances of Italian road law include children under 1.5 m required to be in the back of the car and that a reflective jacket must be worn if your car breaks down on the carriageway in poor visibility. Make sure you've got one. On-the-spot fines for minor traffic offences are not uncommon – typically they range between €150-250. Always get a receipt if you incur one.

Speed limits are 130 kph (motorway), 110 kph (dual carriageway) and 50 kph (town). Limits are 20 kph lower on motorways and dual carriageways when the road is wet. *Autostrade* (motorways) are toll roads, so keep cash in the car as a backup even though you can use credit cards on the blue 'viacard' gates. **Autostrade** ① *T055-420 3200, www. autostrade.it*, provides information on motorways in Italy, and **Automobile Club d'Italia** ① *T06-49981, www.aci.it*, provides general driving information. ACI offers roadside assistance with English-speaking operators on T116.

Be aware that there are restrictions on driving in historic city centres, indicated by signs with black letters ZTL (*zona a traffico limitato*) on a yellow background. If you pass these signs, your registration number may be caught and a fine will wing its way to you. If your hotel is in the centre of town, you may be entitled to an official pass – contact your hotel or car hire company. However, this pass is not universal and allows access to the hotel only.

Car hire Car hire is available at all of Italy's international airports and many domestic airports. You are usually better off booking the car before you arrive in the country, and it's certainly best to do so for popular destinations and at busy times of year. Check in advance the opening times of the car hire office.

Car hire comparison websites and agents are a good place to start a search for the best deals. Try www.holidayautos.co.uk, www.easycar.com and www.carrentals.co.uk.

Check what each hire company requires from you. Some companies will ask for an International Driving Licence, alongside your normal driving licence, if the language of your licence is different to that of the country you're renting the car in. Others are content with an EU licence. You'll need to produce a credit card for most companies. If you book ahead, make sure that the named credit card holder is the same as the person renting and driving the car to avoid any problems. Most companies have a lower age limit of 21 years and require that you've held your licence for at least a year. Many have a young driver surcharge for those under 25. Confirm insurance and any damage waiver charges and keep all your documents with you when you drive.

Moped You could also see some of Umbria from a moped: **Umbria in Vespa** ① *www. umbriainvespa.com*, offers tours and rental from a base near Lake Trasimeno.

Where to stay in Perugia, Assisi and Southern Umbria

With an *agriturismo* or villa for rent on nearly every hillside, old town hotels sprucing themselves up and ancient castles and abbeys reinventing themselves as places to stay, there are plenty of good accommodation options in Umbria. *Agriturismi* and villas are difficult to access without your own transport, though some will arrange to pick you up from a station. Staying in one of the major centres, such as Perugia, Spoleto or Orvieto, gives access to a good transport network, including trains north to Florence and south to Rome. Bear in mind, though, that train stations in the region tend to be down on the plain, often a bus journey away from the centres of hill towns. Wherever you are, a car gives you the invaluable freedom to explore, and none of the distances are enormous, though journeys can be slow. Rural accommodation just outside one of the smaller towns with your own transport might be the best of all worlds. Visit www.bellaumbria.net for some good accommodation listings.

Agriturismi

Italy's stay-on-a-farm concept is beginning to mature. Though there are still plenty of places where the accommodation is fairly plain – not much more than a room with a bed – others are moving upmarket and branching out to specialize in cookery courses, wine tasting, horse riding and even dog training. Vineyards are also beginning to get in on the act, with some offering accommodation as well as guided tours.

In order to qualify as an *agriturismo*, places have to produce a certain amount of their own food. Many are organic, and often this means that meals will include homegrown fruit and vegetables and hand-reared meat. Olive oil, wine and honey are almost always local and abundant. Rural accommodation that doesn't also produce its own food used to be called a country house, but has now been reclassified as *turismo rurale*. Prices for *agriturismi* are usually given per person, and start at around €35 per night – more like €50 for the smarter places. Half board is often a good deal: expect to add around €20 per person for a meal that would probably cost at least €30 in a restaurant.

Price codes

Where to stay

€€€€ over €300   €€€ €200-300

€€ €100-200   € under €100

Price codes refer to the cost of a double room in high season.

Restaurants

€€€ over €30   €€ €20-30   € under €20

Price codes refer to the cost of a two-course meal with a drink for one person, including service and cover charge.

Many *agriturismi* close in the winter, and may impose a minimum stay in the summer. Increasing numbers have websites, but the small nature of these businesses means that they can be hard to find. A few of the best are in this guide, but there are hundreds of others: www.en.agriturismo.it, www.agrituristumbria.com/eng or www.agriguida.com are good places to start a search. Local tourist information websites will usually have lists and links too.

Self-catering

Renting a villa gives you the option of more independence and privacy. Many also have swimming pools. For a family or a small number of people the option of a villa can work out cheaper than staying in a hotel; if you are a group of 10 or so, the savings are greater, and there are some spectacular places to stay.

Good websites to search on include www.holidaylettings.co.uk, which has plenty of choice. **Airbnb** ① *www.airbnb.co.uk*, also has a good range.

Hotels

The region's hotels are often not especially stylish; whereas *agriturismi* have revitalized rural tourism, many town hotels have changed little in the last 30 years and are looking rather stale. Some are wonderful grand old relics, however, and others are bucking the trend and becoming chic and modern, using their old spaces in new and creative ways.

Some of the most interesting places to stay are converted buildings such as old abbeys: **San Pietro in Valle** (see page 78) in the Valnerina offers breakfast in the cloisters.

Hotels can be relatively expensive for what you get – expect to pay around €100 a night for a double room with a reasonable level of comfort. Try searching on www.wheretostayinumbria.com.

Si sposa

Going to Italy to get married in Tuscany is now an old story, and a whole industry has grown up around it. In Umbria it's much more unusual, meaning that you may have to work a little harder to find a venue, but also that you may end up feeling more special.

It's not a cheap option, but you'll have a stunningly memorable venue and a backdrop to match. A handful of places are set up for foreign weddings, such as **Villa di Monte Solare** (see page 47), in the hills south of Lake Trasimeno. Some venues have their own chapels, often centuries-old buildings that once served long-abandoned hilltop villages, and the best will organize everything for you – from the service to evening yoga and massage sessions. For some organizational assistance, try Love and Lord, www.loveandlord.com, in the UK.

Food and drink in Perugia, Assisi and Southern Umbria

Food

Umbria is known for its uncomplicated but delicious cuisine. Pasta and gnocchi, usually home-made, are delicious, often served with a simple tomato and wild boar sauce, or with local pecorino cheese. Landlocked Umbria has a proud tradition of cured meat and cheeses, which go excellently well with the crusty, fresh, saltless bread that is traditional here. Freshwater fish and eels from the lakes and rivers are sometimes found on menus too. Lentils are grown locally, especially in the Sibillini Mountains, and grains often feature in soups. Most ingredients are local, often supplied by small, sometimes organic producers. Tasty radicchio, the sweetest tomatoes and peppery rocket will make a fantastic salad, and if you're making a picnic there are plenty of great ingredients to buy.

Aperitivi Increasingly common is the *aperitivo milanese*: an early evening beer, glass of prosecco, or Campari and soda comes with a help-yourself buffet of meats, cheeses, and even plates of pasta. Most places will offer bowls of crisps and peanuts at least.

Meat and fish The wild boar, once an endangered species in the region, has now become a pest in some areas, and even if you don't glimpse them around the wooded hills of the Apennines you will probably see the evidence of their snuffling for food on the ground. Wild boar meat features on many menus, often as sausages, or with *pappardelle* (pasta ribbons). Other cured meats are common too – a shop selling salami and other pork products is known all over Italy as a *norcineria*, after the town of Norcia, famous for its sharp-knived butchers, who once also had a sideline keeping boys' singing voices high.

Inland, you will probably also come across Chianina beef, from a strain of large white cattle, and freshwater fish. Eel is traditional, as is wood pigeon.

Truffles The product Umbria is probably known for above all others is truffles, and there are few restaurants where you won't find them on the menu in some form or other. They are shaved over pasta and used to flavour meat sauces and even liqueurs. Visit a farm in the country and you will probably see truffling tools, and perhaps meet a truffle hound.

The truffle is not just a way of life, but a potentially very lucrative commodity. By weight, truffles are some of the most valuable foodstuffs in the world, and the mystery surrounding them adds to their expensive allure. Nobody is quite sure how or why truffles grow, and they have not yet been successfully farmed. It is known that they grow in relationship with the roots of certain trees – usually oak – but little more.

In the past, male pigs were used to track them down, but this could lead to trouble: as the smell is apparently very similar to that of a female pig, there might be a fight at the end of a successful hunt over who got the truffle. These days, dogs are used, as they are easier to control.

Fresh truffles are difficult to transport, as well as being fiendishly expensive, but you can buy them in jars, under oil, to take home. Cheaper truffle sauces are also available, usually including some porcini mushrooms along with the truffles.

Cheese Cheese in Umbria is mainly pecorino, of which there is a large variety. Made from sheep's milk, or a blend of milk from sheep and goats, its strength varies depending on how long it has been aged. You may find it matured in red wine, to give flavour and a coloured rind. Moist when young, the matured cheese (*stagionato*) becomes increasingly crumbly.

The story goes that the first *formaggio di fossa* ('trench cheese') was created largely by chance, when pecorino was removed from harm's way in wartime and buried underground. Not only does the cheese undergo a special kind of fermentation in these conditions, but in the few places where it is made yeasts have built up over the years that give it a unique flavour. The cheese is kept in straw-lined pits from August to November, when celebrations accompany its pungent unearthing.

Caciotta is a cows' milk cheese, usually milder than pecorino. White and crumbly, it is similar to English Cheshire cheese.

For the best cheese, you should buy either from small delicatessens or big supermarkets with dedicated counters. Some delis are designed more for tourists than locals, and quality can suffer. Watch where the locals go, and ask for a taste – a good shop will be happy to oblige.

Olive oil Some of the best olive oil in Italy is produced in Umbria, and one of the best varieties of olive for oil is the clean, almond-flavoured Frantoio. For the highest quality, look for a fresh, green colour.

The reasons for the high quality of the oil here are mainly climatic. In the foothills of the Apennines, varieties survive that produce less fruit but more flavour. They are, however, also susceptible to the extreme cold weather that is possible here. At well-irrigated, warmer, lower levels, near to Lake Trasimeno, for example, yields are higher but quality may not be so good.

When buying olive oil look for the expiry date, which by Italian law must be two years after it was made. The newer the oil the better – the best time to buy is in November or December when the new pressing has just arrived in the shops.

Biscuits and desserts Umbria is not great for desserts, with a few exceptions. Most towns have a good ice cream maker or two, but in many restaurants desserts will not be home-made. There are, however, some excellent biscuits to look out for. Most commonly, *tozzetti*, a hard, heavy almond biscuit, similar to the Tuscan *cantucci*, are sold along with *vin santo*, into which they should be dipped. Spicy *mostaccioli*, which St Francis allegedly asked for on his deathbed, are another kind of hard biscuit to look out for. *Baci di Assisi* are softer, nutty confections.

A *digestivo* – a glass of something alcoholic to aid digestion – is commonly drunk at the end of a meal. Sweet dessert wines can be very good, and home-made grappa can sometimes be found, along with *amari* – bitter concoctions that supposedly once had medicinal uses. *Nocino*, walnut liqueur, is another to look out for.

Bread Traditionally made without salt, bread in the region tends to come in large loaves, which are sometimes still baked in a traditional wood oven (ask for *pane al forno*). Because it goes stale quickly, it is often bought in half, or even quarter loaves. Yesterday's leftovers are often used to make *panzanella*, a tomato and bread salad. Saltless bread can take some getting used to, but it can also be delicious, allowing the natural sweetness of the grain to emerge. The story goes that saltless bread developed as a reaction to the Salt War against the papacy in the 16th century (see page 112).

Wine Umbria has 11 DOC wines. In the west, Orvieto is known mainly for its white wine, which has undergone something of a renaissance in recent years. Montefalco is famous for its reds. There are plenty more varieties to look out for, however, and vineyards are increasingly opening their doors to visitors.

Montefalco The hills around Montefalco and Bevagna make some of the region's best red wine. The most sought-after is the expensive Montefalco Sagrantino, a rich wine, strong in tannins, that ages well.

Orvieto Wine has been produced here since Etruscan times: there are wine cellars carved into the rock beneath the town that have been in almost constant use for 2500 years (see page 91). The white wine made here these days is crisp, dry and fruity, made mainly from Grechetto and Trebbiano grapes, unlike the sweet wine the town was once famous for. Some red is also made.

Torgiano South of Perugia, this little town is home to the Lungarotti family, who have set up an excellent wine museum (see page 33) with some of their viticulture millions. There's a big range of whites, reds and sparkling wines and they produce a total of 3 million bottles a year. The Rubesco red is rightly popular.

Eating out Most restaurants will offer an *antipasto* (a starter), followed by a *primo* (first course, usually pasta) and a *secondo* (second course, usually meat) with *contorni* (side dishes) and a *dolce* (dessert). Don't feel pressured into having everything, however, or even into sticking to the order – nobody will mind if you just have a second course, or a side dish without the meat, or a salad as a first course. And despite the preponderance of meat – often wild boar, Chianina beef or game – it's usually eaten as a separate course, so vegetarians won't have a hard time finding good food.

Pizzerias, often run by Neapolitans and serving excellent pizzas, are common and are often open later than standard restaurants – usually until 2400 or 0100. Most bars also serve food – Italians rarely drink without eating, and *enoteche* (wine bars) can be great places for a light lunch or supper.

Breakfast is usually a *cornetto* (a sweet croissant, often jam- or custard-filled) grabbed at a café or bar. The standard of breakfast in hotels is usually poor, so you might be better skipping it and going to the local café. *Agriturismi* do much better. Locals eat lunch around 1300. Evenings often start with an *aperitivo* around 1900, followed by supper any time from 2000 or 2100 until around 2300.

Festivals in Perugia, Assisi and Southern Umbria

It can seem at times as if Umbria has more festivals than inhabitants. From major international music festivals to a couple of loosely linked local events in a remote village hall, there is always something going on somewhere. Add to these a rich history of local traditions, often going back many hundreds of years, and you have a busy calendar.

January

Umbria Jazz Winter Associazione Umbria Jazz, piazza Danti 28, Perugia, T075-573 2432, www.umbriajazz.com. In Orvieto, an offshoot of the main Umbria Jazz festival includes a special Mass on New Year's Day, with gospel singers performing in the magnificent cathedral.

Sant'Emiliano (27th) Trevi. The feast day of Trevi's patron saint is marked by a torchlit procession carrying his statue through the streets.

February

Carnevale Carnival is celebrated everywhere; in some places the masked parades and accompanying parties go on for a week.

April

Easter Easter in Assisi is a holy affair, with solemn processions by torchlight on Good Friday.

Coloriamo i cieli Castiglione del Lago, www.coloriamoicieli.com. The town holds a kite festival ('Let's colour the skies') over several days in late Apr or early May.

May

Calendimaggio Assisi, www. calendimaggiodiassisi.it. A medieval festival revolving around competition between the 2 halves of the city, the *Parte di Sopra* (upper part) and the *Parte di Sotto* (lower part), which plays itself out in dance, theatre, archery and flag-waving over 2 or 3 days in the 1st half of the month.

Corsa all'Anello Narni, www.corsallanello. it. Narni's biggest festival climaxes on the 2nd Sun in May and involves medieval dressing up, baroque music, wine drinking

and a joust where riders try to drive their lances through a ring. The event commemorates the writing of the medieval town's first laws in 1371.

June

Mercato delle Gaite Bevagna, www. ilmercatodellegaite.it. This new week-long festival around the middle of the month celebrates old customs: traditional work practices such as paper- and candle-making are recreated, in the obligatory medieval costumes.

L'Infiorata Spello. On the Sun nearest 21 Jun, Spello is given over to flower power when it hosts a festival in which the streets are decorated with works of art made entirely from thousands of petals.

Festival dei Due Mondi Spoleto, www. festivaldispoleto.com. This classical music festival in Jun and Jul celebrates American and European music (hence the 2 worlds of the title). Outdoor concerts have a stunning setting in the piazza in front of the cathedral.

July

Trasimeno Blues Lago Trasimeno, www.trasimenoblues.it. A week-long programme at the end of Jul featuring international blues artists performing in various locations around the lake.

Umbria Film Festival Montone, www. umbriafilmfestival.com. The 2nd week of the month sees a screen erected in the piazza for the town's bijou film festival, subtitled 'Alternative Voices in European Cinema'. It's no Cannes, but there can be few more idyllic spots to watch films alfresco.

Umbria Jazz Piazza Danti 28, Perugia, T075-573 2432, www.umbriajazz.com. One of the world's biggest jazz festivals, Perugia's annual musicfest is a joyous jamboree, and a festival that many other places in the region have tried to copy. The whole town is completely taken over, and accommodation and decent restaurant tables can be hard to come by. New Orleans bands march through the streets, Italian groups cover Frank Sinatra classics outside the cathedral and American songstresses wail in the piazzas, while bigger names play ticketed gigs in the stadium. It's a great experience if you can find somewhere to stay: the city buzzes and the atmosphere is genial. The jazz theme is often stretched a little – in the past, REM have headlined.

August

Ferragosto National holiday on 5 Aug celebrating the harvest and end of hard labour in the fields and the holy day for Assumption of the Blessed Virgin Mary. The entire month is often taken as a holiday with offices, shops and businesses reopening in Sep.

Palio dei Terzieri (15th) Città della Pieve, www.paliodeiterzieri.it. A day after Gubbio's medieval shenanigans in northern Umbria, something very similar happens in Città della Pieve, where they dust down their flags, crossbows and costumes again for a day of competition between 3 teams. The town's fountain flows with wine as part of the celebrations.

September

Sagra Musicale Umbra Perugia, T075-572 2271, www.perugiamusicaclassica.com. A long-running and well-respected season of sacred music in Perugia and other Umbrian towns, with international artists playing in churches and theatres.

Settimana Enologica Montefalco, www.settimanaenologica.it. A week-long celebration of Sagrantino di Montefalco, with tastings of the new wine, released 3 years after the grapes were harvested.

Todi Festival www.todiartefestival.com. With everything from 'Todi Rock' – a rather tame attempt to bring heavy metal to the town's piazza – to ballet and classical music, Todi's annual arts festival has a bit of something for everyone.

October

Marcia della Pace www.tavoladellapace.it. Every odd-numbered year, on a Sun near the beginning of Oct, around 200,000 people walk the 24 km from Perugia to Assisi to call for peace in the world.

Eurochocolate Perugia, www.euro chocolate.com. What ought to be a great celebration of chocolate tends to lack much in the way of cocoa soul: the commercial massively outweighs the interesting. But it does have its attractions, such as the chance to buy massive amounts of chocolate, or to play giant chocolate chess in front of an audience in piazza IV Novembre.

Essentials A-Z

Accident and emergency
Ambulance T118; **Fire** T115; **Police** T113 (with English-speaking operators), T112 (*carabinieri*); **Roadside assistance** T116.

Electricity
Italy functions on a 220V mains supply. Plugs are the standard European 2-pin variety.

Health
Comprehensive travel and medical insurance is strongly recommended for all travel. EU citizens should apply for a free European Health Insurance Card (www.ehic.org), which has replaced the E111 form and offers free or reduced-cost medical treatment.

Medical services
Late-night pharmacies are identified by a large green cross outside: call T1100 for addresses of the 3 nearest open pharmacies. The accident and emergency department of a hospital is the *pronto soccorso*. The main hospital in Perugia is the Azienda Ospedaliera di Perugia, via Enrico dal Pozzo, T075-578 2861.

See also individual town and city directories throughout the book for details of local medical services.

Language
In hotels and bigger restaurants, you'll usually find English is spoken. The further you go from the tourist centres, however, the more trouble you may have, unless you have at least a smattering of Italian.

Italians from the rest of the country often consider modern-day Umbri to speak with a rather slow, rural accent, and though such attitudes are exaggerated, you may be able to detect a country lilt to some spoken language in the region. That said, it's seldom hard to understand.

Umbrian as an ancient language was one of the prime influences of Latin, but it died out nearly 2000 years ago and few if any of its linguistic traces survive. Umbro dialect still exists, especially in rural areas, and sometimes in the names of traditional local dishes.

Money → *For exchange rates see www.xe.com.*
The Italian currency is the euro. There are ATMs (*bancomat*) throughout Italy that accept major credit and debit cards. To change cash or travellers' cheques throughout Umbria, look for a *cambio*. Many restaurants, shops, museums and art galleries will take major credit cards. Paying directly with debit cards such as Cirrus is less easy in many places, so withdrawing from an ATM and paying in cash may be the better option. Keep some cash for toll roads if you're driving.

Cost of living
Staying in a cheap agriturismo and eating picnics, you could just about get by on €75 a day per person. Double that for a more comfortable holiday, with swimming pool, truffles and Sagrantino.

When visiting tourist attractions you can often buy combined tickets that let you into several sights, though the savings aren't always great. Students and children usually go half price.

Opening hours
Most shops and tourist attractions close at lunchtime. Almost no shops open on Sun and museums are often closed on Mon.

Safety
The crime rate in Italy is generally low, though rates of petty crime are higher. Umbria is generally very safe. Take care when travelling: don't flaunt your valuables; take only what money you need and split

it; don't take risks you wouldn't at home. Beware of scams and con-artists, and don't expect things to go smoothly if you partake in fake goods. Car break-ins are common, so always remove valuables. Take care on public transport, where pickpockets or bag-cutters operate. Earthquakes are a possibility – if you experience one, stay in the open if possible or, if not, shelter in a doorway.

Time
Italy uses Central European Time, GMT+1.

Tipping
Only in the more expensive restaurants will staff necessarily expect a tip, although everyone will be grateful for one; 10-15% is the norm, and it's increasingly common for service to be included in your bill on top of the cover charge. When you're ordering at the bar a few spare coins may speed service up. Taxis may add on extra costs for luggage, but an additional tip is always appreciated.

Rounding up prices always goes down well, especially if it means avoiding giving change – not a favourite Italian habit.

Tourist information
Even small towns have tourist information offices, where you can get a map and advice on the best sights. Most also have lists of accommodation. *Agriturismi* (see page 11) are worth booking before you arrive (www.agrituristumbria.com).

In the university towns, look out for student-produced information. Perugia's *The Little Blue What To Do* (in English, http://inperugia.com) is especially useful; www.livingitalytours.com offers a wealth of historical and cultural information, plus tours.

Visas
UK and EU citizens do not need a visa, but will need a valid passport to enter Italy. A standard tourist visa for those outside the EU is valid for up to 90 days.

Contents

Footprint features

Central Umbria

9/2245153

Perugia, Assisi and Lago Trasimeno

A heady mix of jazz, religion, history, art, hills and food: central Umbria has all of the region's signature features. Perugia, capital of the region and the area's only real city, is a buzzing place, where a cosmopolitan student population gives a sense of fun and energy to a stunningly unspoilt medieval centre, with winding streets and worn stone steps leading down from grand piazzas to Etruscan stone gates.

Not far away across the plain, Assisi, home of St Francis, is a holy town with plenty to offer believers and non-believers alike. Giotto's frescoes in the basilica are said to have rewritten the history of art, and aside from the saints and medieval churches there are also plenty of less obvious pleasures, such as great views across the Umbrian countryside. Even here – the one place in the region that tourism sometimes threatens to overwhelm – it's not hard to find everyday life going on in the back streets.

Lago Trasimeno, a huge glittering expanse of shallow water to the west of the area, has a distinctive cuisine based on its freshwater fish, as well as its own landscape, with ancient islands to explore and walks and cycle routes to blow the cobwebs away.

Perugia → For listings, see pages 45-56.

Capital of the region, and its largest and best-connected city, Perugia is in many ways an anomaly. Its Italian and international universities give it a young, cosmopolitan and lively feel, and its status and size mean that the outskirts, at least, have some of the trappings of modernity. The old centre, however, is as impressive a collection of medieval architecture as you will find anywhere, and the views, when they are visible from the tall, arched streets, are stunning. The city tops several ridges of a hill, and from good vantage points you can see half of Umbria, including Monte Cucco, Assisi and the towns to the south – Trevi, Spello and Montefalco.

Perugia is an intoxicating mix. It's the home of Italy's most famous chocolate, its best jazz festival and one of its best Renaissance painters; it's less pastoral than many of its hill-town neighbours, but often more exciting too. Next to a wine and cheese shop you'll find the latest iPads for sale, and beside a smart wine bar there may be an artisan brewer, where wrinkled Italians mix with bright-eyed international exchange students.

Arriving in Perugia

Getting around There are two train lines that serve the city. From Stazione Sant'Anna, to the south of piazza Italia, trains on the privately run Ferrovia Centrale Umbria line serve stations north to Umbertide and Città di Castello, and south to Todi. For mainline trains, the main Fontivegge Station (usually just called Perugia – don't get off at Perugia Ponte San Giovanni, or Perugia Università) is further outside the centre, at piazza Vittorio Veneto (1.5 km southwest of piazza Italia); from here the Minimetrò is useful for getting to and from the centre, there are frequent buses, or you could get a taxi.

Getting around Other than getting to and from the station, buses and cars are of little use in the city centre, much of which is closed to traffic, or subject to tortuous one-way routes. There are paid car parks dotted around outside the city walls, where you may also be able to find some free parking.

Perugia's **Minimetrò** ① *Mon-Sat 0700-2120, Sun 0830-2030, €1*, is a hi-tech piece of wizardry that slides passengers in space-age pods up the hill from Fontivegge Station into the centre of town every 2½ minutes. It also goes to the Pian di Massiano parking lot, near the football stadium, where there are some free parking places.

City and long-distance buses (T075-506 7894) depart from the APM bus terminal in piazza Partigiani, and most city services stop at piazza Italia, where there's an information and ticket kiosk. A single trip costs €1.50 (€2 if you pay on the bus), or 10 for €12.90; once validated, tickets last 70 minutes. A 24-hour tourist ticket costs €5.40. Good information (in Italian) on all Perugia's transport options is available on www.umbriamobilita.it.

Tourist information Tourist information office ① *piazza Matteotti 18, Loggia dei Lanari, T075-573 6458, daily 0830-1830*. A useful guide to the city, in English, can be downloaded as a pdf from http://turismo.comune.perugia.it, which also has lots of other information on listings and festivals. If you can understand a little Italian, *Viva Perugia* is an invaluable monthly listings magazine, available from newsstands for €1.

Corso Vannucci and piazza IV Novembre

Filled daily with people taking their evening *passeggiata*, and the focus of the **Umbria Jazz** festival, the stunning corso Vannucci is an elegant catwalk even in quieter times. From piazza Italia at the eastern end, across piazza della Repubblica to piazza IV Novembre, cafés spill out on to the wide pavements, and in summer restaurants set up tables in the middle of the street, which makes a great spot for people watching. For much of the time the street is closed to traffic, which greatly adds to the pleasures of window shopping in the smart boutiques and gazing at the extraordinary Gothic and Renaissance architecture.

At the northern end of the *corso*, on the western side, is the huge and oft-extended Palazzo dei Priori – one of Italy's most stunning town halls. Beyond is piazza IV Novembre, with the *duomo* opposite. The centrepiece, between the two power bases of Church and State, is the Fontana Maggiore, a complex piece of medieval design with scenes depicting everything from the glories of the city to Aesop's fables.

Fontana Maggiore

Symbol of the city, Perugia's Romanesque central fountain was built in the 13th century at the end of a long aqueduct. Designed and made by the father-and-son team of Nicola and Giovanni Pisano, it has mostly survived its 730 years remarkably well. It is one of the most important pieces of sculpture of its time – a beautiful and intriguing piece of work that

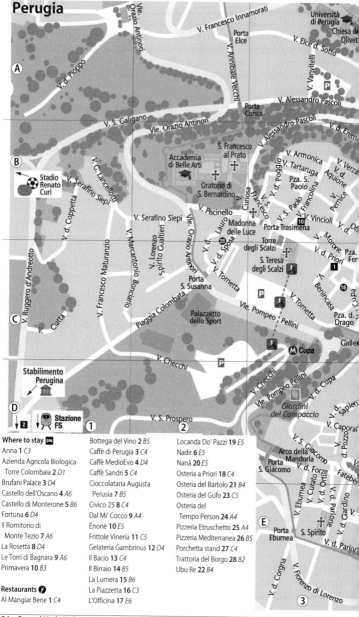

Perugia

Where to stay 🛏

Anna **1** *C3*
Azienda Agricola Biologica
  Torre Colombaia **2** *D1*
Brufani Palace **3** *D4*
Castello dell'Oscano **4** *A6*
Castello di Monterone **5** *B6*
Fortuna **6** *D4*
Il Romitorio di
  Monte Tezio **7** *A6*
La Rosetta **8** *D4*
Le Torri di Bagnara **9** *A6*
Primavera **10** *B3*

Restaurants 🍴

Al Mangiar Bene **1** *C4*
Bottega del Vino **2** *B5*
Caffè di Perugia **3** *C4*
Caffè MedioEvo **4** *D4*
Caffè Sandri **5** *C4*
Cioccolataria Augusta
  Perusia **7** *B5*
Civico 25 **8** *C4*
Dal Mi' Cocco **9** *A4*
Énônè **10** *E5*
Frittole Vineria **11** *C5*
Gelateria Gambrinus **12** *D4*
Il Bacio **13** *C4*
Il Birraio **14** *B5*
La Lumera **15** *B6*
La Piazzetta **16** *C3*
L'Officina **17** *E6*

Locanda Do' Pazzi **19** *E5*
Nadir **6** *E5*
Nanà **20** *E5*
Osteria a Priori **18** *C4*
Osteria del Bartolo **21** *B4*
Osteria del Gufo **23** *C5*
Osteria del
  Tempo Person **24** *A4*
Pizzeria Etruschetto **25** *A4*
Pizzeria Mediterranea **26** *B5*
Porchetta stand **27** *C4*
Trattoria del Borgo **28** *B2*
Ubu Re **22** *B4*

Decoding Perugia's fountain

Starting opposite the Palazzo dei Priori and working anticlockwise, the fountain's lower basin acts as a sort of calendar, with 12 pairs of reliefs each illustrating a month of the year, complete with signs of the zodiac:

January A man and a woman eat by a fire with a jug and a large wine flagon.

February Two fishermen, or perhaps one fisherman shown twice, fishing then going home with the day's catch.

March A figure takes a thorn from his foot and a tree is pruned.

April Ancient Roman figures stand around with branches and flowers.

May A man carrying a bunch of roses pursues a lady on horseback. Look for the dog beneath the woman's horse.

June Hard-working and rather tired-looking peasants gather crops.

July More hard work, this time threshing.

August On an especially decorative panel, two people gather figs.

September Grapes become the centre of attention. In the first panel a bare-legged man crushes them, while in the second another brings more from the vine.

October The wine-making process continues: one barrel is being filled while another is repaired.

November Ploughing and scattering seeds, gathered up in the folds of a cloak. Look for the braying oxen.

December A pig is hung upside-down to be slaughtered, and is subsequently carried away on a shoulder, closely watched by a dog, which tries to jump up.

After December come a lion and a griffin (the city's emblems), four pairs depicting the liberal arts – grammar and dialectics, rhetoric and arithmetic, geometry and music, astronomy and philosophy – and two eagles. The remaining seven pairs represent Adam and Eve, Samson and Delilah, a lion and a man (beating a lion cub), David and Goliath, Romulus and Remus, their she-wolf and Rea Silvia, and two of Aesop's fables: the wolf and the crane, and the wolf and the lamb.

On the fountain's upper level, various religious and historic figures mix with those from Perugia's history. Looking straight down corso Vannucci is **Perugia** herself, as a seated woman holding a basket. On either side of her are personifications of **Chiusi**, with corn, and **Trasimeno**, with some rather slippery-looking fish. Working anticlockwise from here are: **Herculanus** (bishop and patron saint of the city); the **traitor cleric**, who opened the city gates to the Goths in AD 547; **St Benedict**, with St Maurus clasping his thighs; **St John the Baptist**; **King Solomon**; **David** with a small harp; **Salome** with the head of John the Baptist; **Moses** with a tablet; **Matteo** (mayor of Perugia when the fountain was built); **Archangel Michael**; **Eulistes** (mythical founder of Perugia); the priest **Melchisedech**; **Ermanno da Sassoferrato** (capitano del popolo); **Victory**, portrayed as a woman holding a branch; **St Peter** with a key; a woman holding the **Church**; a woman seated and crowned representing **Rome**; a woman with a tablet representing **theology**; **St Paul**; and **St Laurence**, the city's other patron saint.

Finally, the figures at the top of the fountain are the three graces, from whom the water flows, just as it has done for centuries.

repays close inspection. Three figures stand in the middle of two large concentric rings of bas-relief, and the whole thing is a mélange of idealism, romance, symbolism, mythology, religion and significant Perugian figures.

Cattedrale di San Lorenzo

ⓘ *Piazza IV Novembre, T075-572 3832, daily approximately 0700-1300 and 1600-sunset, free.*
Perugia's 15th-century Gothic cathedral dominates one side of piazza IV Novembre, its showiest and most ornate decoration ostentatiously facing the alternative, secular, power base of the Palazzo dei Priori. As well as a 1555 statue of Pope Julius III, there is a pulpit made especially for San Bernardino of Siena when he addressed the city in 1425.

Both the front of the cathedral and its interior fail to live up to the expectations raised by the building's flank, though they are certainly not without interest. The choir stalls and bishop's throne at the front were partially destroyed by fire in 1985, but the original intarsia work of 1486-1491, by Giuliano da Maiano and Domenico del Tasso, has since been carefully restored.

As well as the painted ceiling, the columns in the *duomo* are painted to give a marble effect – look out for the popular shrine to the Madonna delle Grazie on one of them.

In the Cappella di Sant'Anello is the Virgin's supposed wedding ring, said to miraculously change colour depending on who is wearing it. Also here, in the Cappella di San Bernardino, is the 16th-century *Descent from the Cross* by Federico Barocci.

The **Museo Capitolare della Cattedrale di San Lorenzo** ⓘ *T075-572 4853, www. museiecclesiastici.it, Tue-Sun 1000-1300, 1430-1730, €3.50, concession €2.50, under 11s free,* contains 26 rooms of medieval and Renaissance art, including a *Madonna and Child with Saints* by Luca Signorelli. Downstairs, recent excavations have uncovered extensive, if not overly spectacular, Roman remains (guided tour at 1100 or 1530, €5).

Galleria Nazionale dell'Umbria

ⓘ *Corso Vannucci 19, T075-574 1410, www.gallerianazionaleumbria.it, Tue-Sun 0830-1930, audio tour available, €6.50, concession €3.25, EU citizens, under 18s and over 65s free.*
The region's most important art collection is housed in 40 rooms on the upper floors of the Palazzo dei Priori. Good temporary exhibitions are held here, and the highlights of the permanent collection include many works by Perugino and Pinturricchio, as well as an excellent Piero della Francesca.

In chronological order, the collection starts at the top of the building with elements of the town's two 13th-century fountains, including the original three water carriers from the Fontana Maggiore (see page 23). Room 2 has lots of early 14th-century Madonnas, heavy with gold leaf, influenced by Sienese art. In room 4, Maestro di Paciano's figures demonstrate what was to become one of the signature elements of Perugian art: expressive, exaggerated features and faces that are almost caricatures.

Domenico di Bartolo's smooth-faced 1438 polyptych demonstrates an early Sienese appreciation of Renaissance principles in his sense of perspective and the virtuoso way in which he paints the folds of clothes. There's a nice 15th-century dowry chest in room 6, decorated with the story of Tarquin and Lucretia, the former threatening a naked Lucretia with his sword. Also in this room, look for the tiny wild boar in Ottaviano Nelli's five-panel painting of 1403.

By the 1440s, the new figurative reality of the Renaissance had taken hold, and room 8 has pieces commissioned by Perugia's rich and powerful Baglioni family. Fra Angelico's impressive 1448 altarpiece features a Madonna and Child surrounded by St Dominic and St Nicholas on the left, John the Baptist and St Catherine on the right.

Five of the best hidden medieval streets in Perugia

Via dei Priori Through an arch of Palazzo dei Priori, this street apparently once ran red with the blood of medieval family battles.

Via dell'Acquedotto A raised pedestrian walkway created from a 13th-century aqueduct.

Via Roscetto Down winding steps and through arches of various eras.

Corso Garibaldi One of the town's oldest streets, leading out to the northern gate, with prettily painted houses.

Via Volte della Pace A narrow street leading north from piazza Matteotti, this street has more arches than sky.

Gozzoli's 1456 picture features the Madonna with St Peter, John the Baptist, St Paul and St Jerome. Jerome was a cardinal (hence his red hat) who translated the Bible into Latin and, according to medieval stories, removed a thorn from a lion's paw, hence his depiction with a lion in many paintings of the time. The painting shows a three-dimensionality noticeably absent from earlier art – the treatment of the fabrics is especially tactile.

Piero della Francesca's dexterous altarpiece has room 11 to itself, and demonstrates typically virtuoso use of perspective, though the shadows seem strangely miscalculated. The figures on the left are Anthony of Padua and John the Baptist, while on the right are St Francis and Elizabeth of Hungary. The lower predella features the miracles of St Anthony and St Elizabeth. Benedetto Bonfigli's pretty angels offering roses light up room 14, and room 15 has a large Perugino, *The Adoration of the Magi*, from 1523.

Some breaks from religious art are provided at this point, with some fascinating carved ivory mixed with gold pieces in room 17, and wafer irons lining room 20 – these long decorated tongs were used in various parts of Italy but only reached such artistic heights in Perugia, though the best collection of them is in the wine museum in Torgiano (see page 33).

The strongest part of the collection is room 22, where some of Perugino's best works are hung, rich in colour, costumes and light. The *Madonna della Confraternita della Consolazione*, painted in 1496, is particularly beautiful, depicting an especially pensive Virgin with Lake Trasimeno in the background. From here on, however, the Perugino paintings tend to become more formulaic, and it is the Pinturicchio altarpiece from 1495 in room 24 that really catches the eye, with its wonderful details such as the apples and walnuts on the floor and botanically observed studies of plants. The artist designed the whole ensemble, including the Romanesque arches.

The Perugino paintings in room 25 were once part of a huge polyptych, 8 m high, with 30 painted panels that are now scattered around the world. After these come a series of works by his followers, and the collection becomes a little less interesting, though there are some further highlights, such as Orazio Gentileschi's 1618 *Santa Cecilia che suona la spinetta*. Room 39 has historical significance for its images of the Rocca Paolina (see page 31) before it was destroyed.

Collegio del Cambio

ⓘ *Corso Vannucci 25, T075-572 8599, www.collegiodelcambio.it, Mon-Sat 0900-1230, 1430-1730 (closed Mon afternoons Nov to mid-Mar), Sun 0900-1300, €4.50.*

Extraordinary frescoes by Perugino and his assistants are the highlight of these three rooms off the *corso*, though there is intricate intarsia (inlaid wood) work too. The guild of moneychangers was founded in 1259 and moved here in 1457, becoming an important part of city life and taking on the role of a tribunal in financial disputes. The guild still exists today, operating as a charity. They clearly weren't short of a florin or two, hence the expensively commissioned art.

After entering through a room panelled with carved walnut wood you come to the **Sala dell'Udienza**, or council room, frescoed by Perugino from 1498-1500 with the help of his pupils, perhaps including the young Raphael. Its richly colourful paintings, remarkably well conserved, are the Umbrian painter's masterpiece and among the finest Renaissance works in Italy. The schematic design of the paintings was devised by the humanist Francesco Maturanzio, and they pull together the central religious and secular themes of the Renaissance.

Classical figures are represented with personifications of Wisdom, Prudence, Justice, Fortitude and Temperance, while on the end wall the Transfiguration and Nativity are depicted. On the right-hand wall, in perhaps the most successful painting, God looks down on prophets and sybils set in a noticeably central Italian landscape. The figure of Daniel, third from the left, is thought to be a portrait of Raphael. In the centre of the opposite wall, on the painted pilaster, is a self-portrait of Perugino himself, the ostentation of its positioning demonstrating the high regard in which he was held – or, perhaps, in which he held himself.

Don't miss the door through to the **Cappella di San Giovanni Battista**, frescoed with stories of the life of John the Baptist by Perugino's pupil Giannicola di Paola in the early 16th century.

Collegio della Mercanzia
ⓘ *Corso Vannucci 15, T075-573 0366; Mar-Oct and 20 Dec-6 Jan Tue-Sat 0900-1300, 1430-1730, Sun 0900-1300; Nov-Feb Tue and Thu-Fri 0800-1400, 0800-1630, Sun 0900-1300; €4.50.*
Alongside the guild of the moneychangers, the merchants' guild was another important element of medieval Perugian life. This building became its headquarters in 1390 and still oozes wealth and prestige, though it lacks the headlining frescoes of the moneychangers next door. The intricate woodcarving and intarsia work that line the guildhall were carried out in the early 15th century by anonymous artists, perhaps from northern Europe.

Sala dei Notari
ⓘ *Piazza IV Novembre, T075-577 2339, Tue-Sun 0900-1300, 1500-1900, free.*
From the piazza, stone steps curl up to the first floor, where the large and impressive Sala dei Notari was once used for lawyers' meetings. This was the original Palazzo dei Priori, built in the 13th century, before succeeding centuries expanded the building down corso Vannucci. The assembly hall is richly frescoed and beautifully vaulted. Today it is occasionally used for seminars and concerts.

Pozzo Etrusco
ⓘ *Piazza Piccinino 1, T075-573 3669, www.perugiacittamuseo.it, Apr and Aug daily 1000-1330, 1430-1800, May-Jul and Sep-Oct Tue-Sun 1000-1330, 1430-1830, Nov-Mar Tue-Sun 1100-1330, 1430-1700, combined ticket with Cappella di San Severo and Museo delle Porte e delle Mura Urbiche, valid for 7 days, €3.*
Perugia's oldest well is a dank, seeping, dripping place, an enormous work of engineering but also somewhat oppressive: inviting for potholers but less enticing for others. Built in the third or fourth century BC, it held as much as 450,000 litres of water – enough to supply the whole city – and is 3 m in diameter at the bottom, 4.5 m at the top. A chain of buckets on a rope would have been used to collect the water, suspended from the large stone beam across the top. These days water is pumped out electronically to stop the well

A walk around the streets of Perugia

For a city of 160,000 people, Perugia has a remarkably unspoilt historical centre, with labyrinthine medieval streets full of relics of even earlier times.

This hour-long walk around the old centre starts in the heart of the city, **corso Vannucci**. Go under the **Arco dei Priori**, in the middle of Palazzo dei Priori. The street of the same name runs downhill through ancient medieval Perugia. This street is famous for the blood that reputedly ran down it in medieval times, when Perugia's leading families were, quite literally, always at each other's throats.

At the bottom of the street, the **Oratorio di San Bernardino** has a beautiful 15th-century multicoloured bas-relief façade. Next door, the large, pastel-coloured façade of the 13th-century **Chiesa di San Francesco al Prato** is just about all that has survived subsidence – the church is currently being restored and turned into a concert venue.

Turn back towards via dei Priori and take the steps on your left, which become via del Poggio. Don't miss the view over the churches to your left. Follow the road as it bends around to the right and becomes via Armonica, and cross a staggered junction past Teatro Morlacchi into **piazza Morlacchi**, named after Francesco Morlacchi, the Italian composer born in Perugia in 1784. The piazza is a favourite student hangout. Cross it and head down via Baldeschi. You'll soon come to wide steps leading down on your left towards **via dell'Acquedotto**.

A narrow pedestrian street that first runs underneath a bridge and then high above the ground between the surrounding buildings, the via dell'Acquedotto is a remnant of a 13th-century acqueduct, 4 km long, that ran from Monte Pacciano to the Fontana Maggiore. It is also a great way to get out to this quiet part of the old centre.

Continue straight along via dell'Acquedotto, cross via Fabretti and continue uphill along the continuation of the old aqueduct, via Fagiano. Steps at the end lead up to via Benedetta – branch right from here to join **corso Garibaldi**, one of Perugia's oldest streets. If you continue to the end of the *corso* you'll find on your right the **Tempio di Sant'Angelo**, a round church from the sixth century, built using 16 ancient Roman columns. Also here is **Porta Sant'Angelo**, the city's biggest medieval gate (see page 31).

Follow corso Garibaldi back south and you'll arrive in piazza Fortebracci, home of the Università per Stranieri and the **Arco Etrusco**. One of several ancient gates in the city, the hulking mass of the Arco Etrusco is the most famous. Originally built by the Etruscans in the third and second centuries BC, it was added to by the Romans 600 years later, when Emperor Augustus literally stamped his authority on the city. Having conquered – largely destroyed – and subsequently rebuilt the city, he had 'Augusta Perusia' inscribed on the gate, renaming the city after himself.

From here, climb up the steep via Ulisse Rocchi to arrive in piazza Danti, at the back of the cathedral. From the piazza, turn north, taking via del Sole and via Prome to the highest point in the centre of Perugia and a great viewpoint over the northern part of the town to the hills beyond.

filling up, and you can walk down slippery steps to stand in the middle of it, on a newly constructed bridge. The well would originally have been even deeper than its current 37 m, but centuries' worth of detritus has built up at the bottom.

Cappella di San Severo

ⓘ *Piazza Raffaello, T075-573 3864. Apr and Aug daily 1000-1330, 1430-1800; May-Jul and Sep-Oct Tue-Sun 1000-1330, 1430-1830; Nov-Mar Tue-Sun 1100-1330, 1430-1700, combined ticket with Pozzo Etrusco and Museo delle Porte e delle Mura Urbiche, valid for 7 days, €3.*

Raphael's first documented fresco, painted around 1505 when he was in his early 20s, decorates this small and starkly plain chapel. Only the top half is Raphael's – he was called away to paint the Vatican and left the fresco unfinished. At the top of the painting God has almost completely disappeared, but underneath, to either side of Jesus, St Maurus, St Placidus, St Benedict the Abbot, Romuald, Benedict the Martyr and John the Monk are colourfully depicted, all with distinctively Raphael noses. After Raphael's death his one-time teacher, Perugino, completed the lower section in 1521, and the similarities and differences between the styles of student and teacher are interesting to study. At the back of the chapel, a 19th-century etching shows what the undamaged fresco once looked like.

Cassero di Porta Sant'Angelo and Museo delle Porte e delle Mura Urbiche

ⓘ *Corso Garibaldi, T075-41670. Apr and Aug daily 1000-1330, 1430-1800; May-Jul and Sep-Oct Tue-Sun 1000-1330, 1430-1830; Nov-Mar Tue-Sun 1100-1330, 1430-1700, combined ticket with Pozzo Etrusco and Cappella di San Severo, valid for 7 days, €3.*

Porta Sant'Angelo, the biggest of the city's medieval gates, houses a rather dusty old museum dedicated to the fortification of Perugia, with dilapidated models of the city. It has some good views. Nearby, the unusual round **Chiesa di Sant'Angelo**, built in the fifth and sixth centuries, is the city's oldest church and incorporates 16 ancient Roman columns in its construction.

Rocca Paolina

ⓘ *Entry from via Marzia, piazza Italia, via Masi or viale Indipendenza, daily 0800-1900, free.*

After the papal victory over the city in the Salt War of 1540, the not altogether placatory response by Pope Paul III was to build an enormous castle right over the top of the area of Perugia where the ruling Baglioni family lived. Hatred of this symbol of domination simmered for centuries until the Perugian population finally took their revenge by pulling the building down in 1859.

In using the existing houses as foundations for his giant fortress, what the pope's project succeeded in doing was preserving the streets below exactly as they were in the 16th century. Under the giant vaults built over the area, many can be walked around now: a sort of latter-day Pompeii, it's a dim, shadowy, atmospheric place that feels full of the ghosts of the past.

More of the fascinating history is told in the **Museo della Rocca Paolina e la Città** ⓘ *T075-572 5778, www.sistemamuseo.it, Apr and Aug daily 1000-1330, 1430-1800; May-Jul and Sep-Oct Tue-Sun 1000-1330, 1430-1800; Nov-Mar Tue-Sun 1100-1330, 1430-1700, €1.*

Palazzo della Penna

ⓘ *Via Podiani 11, T075-571 6233, www.sistemamuseo.com, Apr and Aug daily 1000-1300, 1600-1900; May-Jul and Sep-Oct Tue-Sun 1000-1300, 1600-1900; Nov-Mar Tue-Sun 1030-1300, 1600-1830, €3.*

Perugia's 'modern art' museum has works from the 18th and 19th centuries, as well as a collection of six large sketches by German hero of the 1960s, Joseph Beuys. Bought at great expense by the city when Beuys came to visit in 1980, they are either incoherent doodlings or intriguing insights into his mind, depending on your point of view. The museum has a decent collection of Italian Futurist painting. Temporary exhibitions are held on the first floor.

Museo Archeologico Nazionale dell'Umbria

ⓘ *Piazza Giordano Bruno 10, T075-572 7141, www.archeopg.arti.beniculturali.it, Mon 1000-1930, Tue-Sun 0830-1930, €4.*

Perugia's excellent archeological museum, in the cloisters of San Domenico, is a treasure trove of local finds, most of them pre-Roman. The ground floor, lined with various ancient stone carvings, can be visited without a ticket. For the best bits, however, climb the stairs in the corner to the first floor, where some beautiful carved stone funerary urns line the cloister, and other pieces are displayed inside.

Women in and around Perugia in Etruscan times seem to have been buried with the same dignity as men, and it is noticeable that many of the grander urns, with statues reclining as if for a banquet on the lids, are for women. Indeed the preponderance of single-sex tombs in the area has led to speculation that families may have been buried along matriarchal lines.

In rooms off to the left is a huge collection of amulets from around the world – an anthropological insight into superstition. More interesting are the rooms on the near side of the cloister, where you will find such pieces as a fourth-century BC shield, coins, a prehistoric corridor complete with bones and flints, armour including some rather fetching knee and shin plates, some beautifully decorated funeral pots and delicate gold jewellery. A ceramic pair of breasts and a couple of uteruses would have been used as votive offerings, perhaps during prayers for fertility.

Chiesa di San Pietro

ⓘ *Via Borgo XX Giugno, T075-34770, Mon-Fri 0900-1300, Tue and Thu also 1530-1830, free.*

An extraordinary ensemble of painting, colour and wood wizardry, the Church of St Peter, built in the 10th century, also has beautiful cloisters and is well worth the walk from the centre out to this corner of the city. Among the highlights is an extraordinary choir, where the intarsia work is said by some to be as good as any in Italy, and where each armrest is decorated with a different carved mythological creature. There is a *Pietà* by Perugino on the left wall.

The church's bell tower is one of the most distinctive elements of the city's skyline. San Domenico once had a similar spire at the top of its campanile, but it was demolished in 1540 as it interfered with the view from the Rocca Paolina.

Orto Medievale

ⓘ *Via Borgo XX Giugno, T075-585 6432, Mon-Fri 0800-1700, free.*

The theory behind this little corner of greenery is that it follows medieval thought. In reality it's a slightly strange mix of cosmology, mysticism, numerology and claptrap about the way in which lilies represent 'cosmogonic ovulation', but it's certainly pretty enough to warrant a visit all the same. There's a waterfall, and butterflies and lizards flit between the flowers. The tree of eternal youth, however, is looking rather decrepit.

Galleria Miomao

ⓘ *Corso Cavour 120, T347-783 1708, www.miomao.net, Tue-Sat 1500-2000.*

A contemporary cartoon gallery, Miomao mounts exhibitions of cartoon art from Italy and around the world.

Around Perugia → *For listings, see pages 45-56.*

Ipogeo dei Volumni

ⓘ *Via Assisana, T075-393329, daily Jul-Aug 0900-1230, 1630-1900, Sep-Jun 0900-1300, 1530-1830, €3, about 5 km southeast of Perugia on SS75 towards Ponte San Giovanni.*

The most elaborate of a series of Etruscan graves just outside Perugia, this is the burial place of a rich and important family and dates from the third or second century BC. It was discovered in 1840 while a road was being built, and is the biggest of the 38 tombs found here. Underneath a busy road, it's hardly in the most romantic of positions, and takes some effort to get to, but is worth the trouble for its impressive Etruscan sculpture and for the Tutankhamun-esque feeling you get as you descend the steps into the tomb.

There are seven urns – six Etruscan and one later Roman one. Don't miss the phalluses (symbols of good luck and fertility) at the top of the stairs among a large collection of other urns discovered in the burial ground outside. The earliest tombs here, among the olive trees, date back to the sixth century BC – ancient even in Roman times. There's also an antiquarium containing more interesting, and in one case rather erotic, Etruscan urns.

Perugina chocolate factory

ⓘ *Via San Sisto 42, San Sisto, T075-527 6796, www.perugina.it, Mon-Fri 0900-1300, 1400-1730 (Mar-Sep also Sat morning), telephone to book a visit and tour in English, free; to get there leave E45 at Madonna Alta exit and drive through San Sisto – the factory is on the right.*

The source of all the world's Baci (the factory produces 1.5 million a day, complete with their characteristic multilingual axioms of love), a tour of this huge Willy Wonka-style palace of chocolate is an interesting and enjoyable experience, despite its position in the ugly industrial hinterland of Perugia.

One-hour visits start with a 15-minute 'infomercial' about chocolate in general and the history of Perugina, plus some free tasters, before heading to a museum, and then – the highlight – along a raised walkway above the factory floor, from where you get great views of the chocolate process below, from vat to mould to wrapping.

Should you wish to get closer to the melted chocolate, courses are available at a smart new chocolate school in the building.

Torgiano

Museo del Vino ⓘ *corso Vittorio Emanuele 31, Torgiano, 15 km south of Perugia off SS3bis, T075-988 0200, www.vino.lungarotti.biz; Jul-Sep daily 1000-1800; Apr-Jun Tue-Sun 1000-1300, 1500-1800; Oct-Mar Tue-Sun 1000-1300, 1500-1700; audiotour available; €4.50, concession €2.50, combined ticket with Museo dell'Olivo e dell'Olio €7, concession €4.50.*

Housed in a 17th-century building in the centre of Torgiano, a sleepy place that is home to the wine millionaires of the Lungarotti Foundation, Umbria's best wine museum is a fascinating place, densely packed with artefacts, art, ceramics and paraphernalia relating to the great drink. The museum's claim to be a testament to the civilization of humanity may be a little grand, but it does go far beyond simply demonstrating the wine-making process. Some of the most interesting pieces are the *beve se puoi* ('drink if you can') glasses – complex and ancient novelties that challenge the user to work out how to drink the contents without spilling them. There are also some beautiful ceramic wine jugs from nearby Deruta (see below), some contemporary art collected by the Lungarotti family and a collection of intricately patterned wafer irons.

Museo dell'Olivo e dell'Oli ① *via Garibaldi 10, Torgiano, T075-9880 3300, www.olio. lungarotti.biz; Jul-Sep daily 1000-1800; Apr-Jun Tue-Sun 1000-1300, 1500-1800; Oct-Mar Tue-Sun 1000-1300, 1500-1700; €4.50, concession €2.50, combined ticket with Museo del Vino €7, concession €4.50*. Though it suffers slightly by comparison with its more illustrious sibling, Torgiano's olive oil museum gives an extensive background to everything olive-related, going back to Roman times.

Deruta

Famed for centuries for its majolica, Deruta, 19 km south of Perugia on E45/SS3bis, is the place to come should you want a white-glazed olive oil pourer entwined with colourful fruit. The whole town can feel a little like a giant ceramics bazaar, but once you're in the small centre, away from the giant ceramics outlets near the motorway, it's not an unattractive place, and in among the gaudy replicas of age-old designs it's possible to find some better quality pieces.

Just south of the town, the **Museo Regionale della Ceramica** ① *largo San Francesco, T075-971 1000, Apr-Jun daily 1030-1300, 1500-1800, Jul-Sep daily 1000-1300, 1530-1900, Oct-Mar Wed-Mon 1030-1300, 1430-1700, €5*, illustrates the history of its principal industry.

The most bizarre use of Deruta's pottery is 2 km south at the **Chiesa della Madonna dei Bagni** ① *daily, summer 0730-1230, 1430-1900, winter 0800-1230, 1430-1830*. Here every wall is covered with colourful glazed tiles commemorating miraculous escapes from dramatic deaths, from a man who fell off his horse in 1701, to someone who was electrocuted while working on a pylon in 1971 and a motorway pile-up in 2000.

Monte Tezio

Most of Perugia's immediate surroundings are low-lying and rather built up. To the north, however, 961-m Monte Tezio, 13 km north of Perugia, offers a quick and easy trip into rural Umbria. From Cenerente, 5 km northwest of Porta Sant'Angelo, a road to the right climbs towards Migiana di Monte Tezio. Just before you reach Migiana, a waymarked but sometimes overgrown path off to the left leads to the summit, a couple of hours' walk. For better tended paths, turn left off the road about 1 km before Migiana and follow the route up the valley of the Fosso di Migliana via the ex-hermitage of Romitorio.

Assisi → *For listings, see pages 45-56.*

Perched high above the flat valley floor, on the flank of Monte Subasio, Assisi must have been a spectacular place even before the creation of so many extraordinary buildings and frescoes in veneration of its favourite son, St Francis. Cobbled streets wind across the hill, with occasional big views past geranium-filled window boxes to the valley below. Cats laze in the sun, nuns and monks climb stone stairs, and tour guides snake their parties through narrow streets. In high summer Assisi teems with tourists and pilgrims, but many of these arrive late and leave early, making the evenings and mornings relatively peaceful.

St Francis

Environmentalist and patron saint of just about everything, from animals to Italy, St Francis's effect on Christianity has been enormous, and he is widely accepted as the most important of the pantheon of Christian saints; by Franciscans, he is revered on a par with Jesus.

One of seven children, Francesco di Bernardone was born to a wealthy cloth merchant of Assisi in 1181. His French mother Pica had him baptised Giovanni in his father Pietro's absence on business in France, but when Pietro returned he decided to rename him Francesco. At the age of 20, Francesco took part in an unsuccessful military raid on Perugia; he was captured there, and the meditative year he spent in prison probably had a profound effect on him.

Back in Assisi, while praying in the crumbling Chiesa di San Damiano (see page 42), Francis had a vision of Christ asking him to repair his house. Taking the instruction literally, he sold his possessions to help repair the church. His father was incensed by this and threatened to disinherit him, but Francis publicly renounced his inheritance and all his worldly goods, discarding even the clothes he was standing in, and embraced poverty as the way to godliness.

Never ordained as a priest, he lived a simple but cheerful life wandering through the woods, hills and mountains of Umbria, singing and preaching. Later, having met Pope Innocent III and received official recognition and permission to found a new religious order, he travelled to Egypt to intervene non-violently in the Crusades, and had an audience with Sultan Melek-el-Kamel, who was so impressed by his faith that he allowed him to preach to his subjects.

In the town of Greccio, near Assisi, Francis set up the first-known three-dimensional Nativity scene. But it is his poetry and writings, mostly written in Umbrian dialect rather than Latin because he believed in communicating with ordinary people, that have proved his most lasting epitaph. Often expressing his love towards the natural world, they offered a new path for Christianity at a time when it was increasingly tottering under the weight of corruption.

Arriving in Assisi

Getting there There are trains every hour or so from Perugia to Assisi (20 minutes). Coming from the south, main line trains from Rome to Ancona stop at Foligno, where you can change for Assisi (15 minutes).

Getting around Traffic is restricted in the centre, and parking is limited to an hour. There are car parks outside the walls, with free parking outside Porta San Giacomo. The train station, Santa Maria degli Angeli, is around 3 km southwest of the city walls. A taxi into the centre costs around €10. You can get a bus from the station to piazza Matteotti, in the city centre (buy a ticket in the bar for €1 or for €1.50 on board, where you'll need the correct change). Buses run half-hourly but sometimes wait for incoming trains. Two other routes run from the main car parks outside the walls into the centre.

Tourist information Tourist information office ① *piazza del Comune, T0758-12534, Mon-Sat 0800-1400, 1500–1800, Sun 0900-1300.*

Basilica di San Francesco

ⓘ *Piazza San Francesco, T075-819001, www.sanfrancescoassisi.org, daily, lower church Easter-Nov 0600-1845, Nov-Easter 0600-1745; upper church, Easter-Nov 0830-1845, Nov-Easter 0830-1745, free.*

Umbria's one truly unmissable sight, the Basilica of St Francis is a many-tiered jewel box on the side of a hill. Large yet intimate, bold yet intricate, it leaves few visitors cold. And though there are many visitors, it's surprisingly easy to avoid the worst crowds by going early in the morning or later in the evening, when the extraordinary beauty of

Assisi

Where to stay 🛏		Restaurants 🍴
Agriturismo Alla Madonna del Piatto **1**	Castello di Petrata **3**	Caffè del Lion d'Oro **1**
	Il Palazzo **4**	Caffè Duomo **2**
Brigolante Guest Apartments **2**	Pallotta **5**	Gran Caffè **3**
	San Crispino **6**	La Fortezza **4**
	Subasio **7**	

the place is easier to appreciate. Evenings have the advantage of great sunsets over the Umbrian plains.

Frescoed with some of Italy's finest paintings and lit through extraordinary stained glass, the basilica is a colourful and uplifting place, and a suitable celebration of St Francis – much more so than the dour sterility of the huge Santa Maria degli Angeli (see page 42) down on the plain. Byzantine influences meld with Gothic and Romanesque architecture to stunning effect, and the restorations after the damage caused by the 1997 earthquake have left the church in fine fettle.

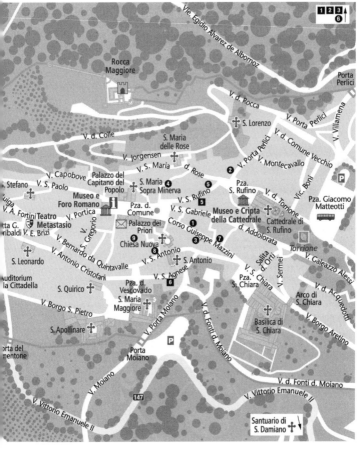

The 1997 earthquake

When earthquakes shook Umbria and Marche in September 1997, many were made homeless and the cathedrals in Orvieto and Urbino were damaged. But it was scenes recorded on a video camera inside the basilica in Assisi that made the news headlines. A first earthquake struck, measuring 5.6 on the Richter scale. However, worse was to come – 10 hours later a second quake, more powerful than the first, struck just as a group of experts were examining the earlier damage to the basilica. People inside the church described how they looked up and saw pieces of the building falling towards them. Four people in the basilica were killed by falling masonry.

The subsequent US$50 million restoration was a painstaking two-year process, piecing together tens of thousands of tiny fragments of frescoes by Cimabue and Giotto. Some think the money spent on the basilica could have been better directed towards helping those made homeless by the earthquake. Even today, work continues to rebuild the nearby town of Nocera Umbra.

There are in fact two churches here – one on top of the other. Construction of the lower church started immediately on the canonization of St Francis, just 18 months after his death in 1226. His body was brought here in 1230. The upper church was begun soon after, and was finished in 1253. The hill on which the church sits was previously a place where criminals were executed and buried and was known as the Colle d'Inferno – the 'hill of hell'; it was where St Francis had asked to be buried.

Basilica Inferiore Entered down stairs from the main façade, through a beautiful double doorway under a rose window, the lower church is a sepulchral basilica. In the crypt here is the tomb of St Francis himself.

The wooden doors are carved with stories from the lives of St Francis, St Clare, St Louis and St Anthony, added in the 16th century. Inside, chapels open off either side of a central nave with semicircular arches, richly patterned. The frescoes in the nave are by an unknown artist, known as the Maestro di San Francesco. Significantly, they illustrate five scenes from the life of Christ on the right side, and five scenes from the life of St Francis on the other: the juxtapositioning and the equal weighting constitute a deliberate move to equate one with the other.

The so-called *Madonna dei Tramonti (Our Lady of the Sunset)* by Pietro Lorenzetti, created between 1315 and 1330, is a beautiful painting that catches the evening light. It controversially seems to show Mary suggesting to Jesus that St Francis should be preferred to St John the Baptist.

Other highlights include the Chapel of Mary Magdalene, with frescoes by Giotto (1307-1308) illustrating her life, and Lorenzotti's pictures of Christ and St Francis in the presbytery and apse.

Tomba di San Francesco Down another level, the tomb of St Francis was never designed to be on public display, but the ground around it was dug out in the early 20th century, leaving a central column within which his body rests. It is a sombre but strangely modern place, and, though many clearly appreciate the opportunity to pay their respects, one can't help but feel that St Francis himself would not have wanted it this way.

Basilica Superiore After the relatively dark and sombre lower basilica, the upper church is a palace of light and colour. Giotto's 28 frescoes around the nave, illustrating episodes from the life of St Francis, demonstrate a rare perception of emotion as well as of perspective, very different to other art of the time. With their backgrounds and their understanding of three-dimensional space, they broke new artistic ground and paved the way for the Renaissance.

Clockwise from the far north side (to the right of the altar), they depict: Francis being honoured by a man who lays down his cloak for him; Francis giving his cloak to a poor man; Francis's dream of a palace filled with arms; the image of Christ in the Church of St Damian asking Francis to repair his church; Francis stripping off and renouncing his worldly goods; Pope Innocent III dreaming that Francis is saving the church from collapse; the Pope confirming Francis's order; the vision of the fiery chariot; the vision of the heavenly thrones; Francis expelling the devils from war-torn Arezzo; Francis offering to walk through fire in front of the sultan; the ecstasy of Francis; Francis creating his crib at Greccio – supposedly the world's first; the miracle of the spring; Francis preaching to the birds; the death of the knight of Celano; Francis preaching to Pope Honorius III; the apparition of Francis to the friars of the chapter at Arles; Francis receiving the stigmata; the death of Francis; Francis appearing in the visions of Fra Agostino and the bishop of Assisi; the recognition of the stigmata; Clare grieving over the body of Francis; the canonization of St Francis; the apparition of St Francis to Pope Gregory IX; the healing of John of Ylerda; the confession of a woman brought back to life; and Francis liberating a repentant heretic.

A plaque just inside the door commemorates the 1997 earthquake, which killed four people here in the basilica when large parts of the vaulting, some frescoed by Cimabue, collapsed.

Cimabue's work has also fared badly elsewhere in the upper church. The apse and western end of the transept feature frescoes painted in the late 13th century by the Florentine artist and his workshop. Due to deterioration caused by the use of lead oxide in his paint, which was probably applied to plaster that wasn't fresh enough, the paintings have a strange, ghostly, negative effect, rather like solarized photographs. Enough is visible, however, especially in his *Crucifixion*, to retain an impressive sense of drama.

The 13th-century Gothic windows, richly decorated with geometric patterns, are some of the finest in the region, and may have been made by a French, German or English artist.

Via San Francesco

Winding its way from the basilica to the piazza del Comune (by which time it has become via Portica), via San Francesco is the nearest Assisi comes to having a main street. Dominated by overpriced ice cream and souvenir shops at the basilica end, it slowly takes on more of the medieval feel of the town, and it has a couple of worthwhile sights along its route – the art gallery and the sumptuously frescoed Oratorio dei Pellegrini.

Pinacoteca Comunale di Assisi

ⓘ *Via San Francesco 12, T075-812033, www.sistemamuseo.it, daily Jun-Aug 1000-1300, 1430-1900; Mar-May, Sep and Oct 1000-1300, 1430-1800; Nov-Feb 1030-1300, 1400-1700, €5, concession €3.50.*

Assisi's picture gallery has a number of exceptional paintings, such as Giotto's *Virgin and Child Enthroned*, painted around 1305 and demonstrating a rare spatial awareness. Perugino's *Virgin and Child* of 1477 has a motherly tenderness, in marked contrast to the stylized and relatively primitive forms of the previous room.

Downstairs, changing exhibitions vary wildly, from the cutesy (nativity scenes) to the gory (the martyring of saints).

Oratorio dei Pellegrini

ⓘ *Via San Francesco 11, T075-812267, Mon-Sat 1000-1200, 1600-1800, free.*

A small square chapel built in 1457 for pilgrims coming to Assisi, the oratory contains some lovely, colourful 15th-century frescoes by Matteo da Gualdo, Pier Antonio Mezzastris and Andrea di Assisi, a student of Perugino. Nearly every inch of the walls is frescoed: da Gualdo's Mary and a baby Jesus are behind the altar, with St James to the left and St Anthony Abbot to the right. Angels around them play musical instruments and sing. Stories from the life of St Anthony Abbot are illustrated on the left wall, opposite stories of St James, including one about a roast chicken that came back to life to stand witness against a judge who had condemned an innocent man to death. The vaults above feature St Gregory, St Ambrose, St Jerome and St Augustine.

Foro Romano e Museo Archeologico

ⓘ *Via Portica 2, T075-813053, Jun-Aug 1000-1300, 1430-1900; Mar-May, Sep and Oct 1000-1300, 1430-1800; Nov-Feb 1030-1300, 1400-1700, €4, concession €2.50*

One of the best archaeology collections around, Assisi's redesigned and renovated museum is displayed in the Roman Forum itself, under the town's central piazza and surrounding streets. The museum has been expertly spruced up – it is well lit and intelligently laid out, and it has good information boards in English.

Among the fragments of Roman inscriptions in stone in the first room is an arresting phallus, symbol of fertility and good luck. Also here, distinctive Roman funeral urns from Assisi display six-petalled flowers.

A glass-floored walkway runs over Roman paving and a drain, with archaeological finds displayed right and left.

The tribunal is a U-shaped limestone podium, probably used for public speaking. Holes in the surface would have held metal benches. Only the base remains of the aedicule, from the first century AD, but there are some beautiful inscriptions. Walking around it, on the paving stones worn down by thousands of pairs of Roman sandals, it's possible to imagine yourself in Roman Asisium 2000 years ago. A magnificently engineered wall, with barrel-vaulted monumental fountains, runs along what would have been the northern side of the forum; on the eastern side are what would have been shops.

A projected video is well worth watching for its three-dimensional virtual reconstructions of how the centre of the Roman town once looked.

Santa Maria Sopra Minerva

ⓘ *Piazza del Comune, Mon and Wed-Thu 0715-1900, Tue and Fri 0715-1400, 1515-1900, Sat-Sun 0815-1900, free.*

Piazza del Comune, Assisi's central piazza, is usually filled with tourists leaving, arriving, trooping in and out of the tourist information office, or sitting having a drink at one of the cafés. The church here is remarkable for its portal, which is the front section of the ancient Roman temple of Minerva. The building features prominently in one of Giotto's frescoes in the Basilica di San Francesco (see page 36).

The temple was built here in the first century BC, financed by two private citizens of Assisi. From the sixth century it was used by Benedictine monks, until in the 13th century it became the town hall. In 1539, Pope Paul III ordered that it should be restored as a church and dedicated to the Virgin Mary, and it was later entrusted to a Franciscan order. After the splendid façade, however, the baroque interior is a disappointment.

Opposite the church is a vaulted passage with some rather rude Roman frescoes on its underside. Recently restored, these once advertised the way to Assisi's brothels.

Basilica di Santa Chiara

ⓘ *Piazza Santa Chiara 1, T075-812282, daily 0700-1200, 1400 till sunset, free.*

At the opposite end of Assisi to St Francis's basilica, his counterpart St Clare has a striking church, with a large rose window, flying buttresses, and a piazza at the front with great views across the Umbrian plain.

Inside there are many rather damaged, and not especially well lit, frescoes, especially on the rib-vaulted ceiling above the altar. Note the two different depictions of Jesus on the cross: one calm, one very much suffering – these were the result of much religious debate and hand-wringing as to whether Jesus felt pain or not.

Down in the crypt, Clare's body can be seen in her tomb, and a glass cabinet displays her cloak and locks of her hair, together with the cloak of St Francis. Born in Assisi to a noble family, Clare renounced her wealth to follow the example of Francis, eventually setting up a convent at San Damiano and founding the order known as the Poor Clares.

Cattedrale di San Ruffino

ⓘ *Piazza San Rufino, T075-812283, www.assisimuseodiocesano.com, daily summer 0700-1300, 1430-1800, winter 0700-1300, 1500-1900, free.*

The façade of Assisi's 12th-century cathedral, in three sections as is often the case in Umbria, is a fascinating storyboard, populated with weird and wonderful creatures – winged serpents, griffins, and lions in the process of devouring a sheep and a man. There's even a small dog trotting down the façade, to the right of the ornate rose window.

The large, pale interior of the cathedral is less interesting. Many come to see the font in which St Francis and St Clare were baptized, to the right inside the entrance, but more impressive is the large Roman cistern opposite, next to the exit. There are more, rather indistinct, Roman remains under glass down the centre of the aisle and further archeological fragments in the museum in the **crypt** ⓘ *Mar-Oct 1000-1300, 1500-1800, Nov-Feb 1000-1300, 1430-1730, €3.50.*

Rocca Maggiore

ⓘ *T075-812033, www.sistemamuseo.it, daily Jun-Aug 0900 till sunset, Sep-May 1000 till sunset, €5.*

On the hill above Assisi, the town's castle has had many incarnations. There's almost certainly been some kind of fort here since pre-Roman times, but most of the current building dates from Cardinal Albornoz's construction on behalf of the papacy in the 14th century. It's not a beautiful building, but there are some great views from the top and a thrillingly long passageway between its two towers. You can climb the northwest tower by a new metal spiral staircase, but the best views are from the top of the polygonal tower, 105 m away, reached along a narrow corridor, lit by slit windows and lamps. Part of the castle is used as a temporary exhibition space.

Abbazia di San Pietro

ⓘ *Piazza San Pietro, T075-812311, daily 0730-1900.*

A strikingly stark Romanesque church, San Pietro has an almost completely bare stone and brick interior, but its light and sense of open space means that it avoids seeming austere. It has hardly changed since the almost square façade was completed in 1268. The three rose windows and a few slim stained-glass windows pinprick the walls with colour – look too for the fragments of mosaic on the ceiling buttresses. The early influence of Gothic architecture shows in the tops of its arches, which have the merest suggestion of points, and in the centre of the nave there is a splendid brick dome. At the front of the building, two rather weathered lions guard the handsome entrance.

Chiesa di San Damiano

ⓘ *Daily Nov-Mar 1000-1200, 1400-1630, Apr-Oct 1000-1200, 1400-1800, free, go through Porta Nuova and follow signs down hill for about 1 km.*

Outside Assisi's walls to the southeast, down a flowery path flanked by olive groves, San Damiano is a peaceful place. It was here in 1205 that St Francis is supposed to have received the call to repair the church, and here that St Clare lived, and died. Francis came to church to visit her just once, though his body was kept here for a while after death.

The small cloister has flowers and a central well, and you can lean over to see into the refectory, with its original wooden benches and frescoed end wall. Through the church you pass the Coretto (choir), a small square room with an arched ceiling, and up the stairs is the Oratorio, a small chapel, richly frescoed. Beyond this is the dormitory – in the corner a simple cross marks the site of Clare's death.

Basilica di Santa Maria degli Angeli

ⓘ *Santa Maria degli Angeli, T075-80511, www.porziuncola.org, daily 0615-1230, 1430-1930, free, 4 km west of Assisi, down on the plain.*

When St Francis abandoned his possessions (and his clothes) and left Assisi, he came here, to a tiny chapel in the woods. The chapel survives, and if you squint very hard it is just about possible to imagine St Francis here, living a simple life and talking to the birds. Open your eyes a little wider, however, and you will see an enormous basilica surrounding the cowering **Porziuncola**, which looks like a dolls' house in comparison to the gargantuan monstrosity built over its head.

St Francis founded his order of friars here, and died here in 1226, but it wasn't until the 16th century that Pope Pius V decided that something more befitting the grandeur of the church should be built around the popular pilgrimage spot. Work began on the basilica in 1568 and was eventually finished in 1684. At 116 m long it is one of the largest basilicas in the world.

Despite the way in which a humble life dedicated to simplicity is celebrated with such ostentation and ornamentation, it's well worth a visit to see Francis's chapel. The paintings, inside and out, have been added since his death. The altar, notably, was painted by Ilario da Viterbo in 1393.

In the **Cappella del Transito** (Chapel of the Transition), the infirmary of the friary where Francis died, after having asked to be placed on the ground, there is a statue of the saint by Andrea della Robbia from 1490. The internal frescoes were painted by Giovanni Spagna in 1520.

The **Museo della Porziuncola** ⓘ *T075-805 1430, daily 0900-1230, 1500-1800*, also has some interesting exhibits, including a 13th-century painting of St Francis and works by Tiberio d'Assisi.

Parco del Monte Subasio

ⓘ *T075-815 5290, www.parks.it, road open until 2100 in summer, 1900 in winter.*

Winding up through Assisi's porta Cappuccini and across the wooded slopes beyond, the Monte Subasio road becomes a wide, stony track that opens out on to the grassy uplands above the tree line. Monks follow St Francis's paths, paragliders step off the edge into the sky and visitors gulp at the gargantuan views. Monte Subasio, wild and craggy, snow-topped for some of the year, is a world apart from the lace shops and postcards of Assisi below.

Lago Trasimeno → *For listings, see pages 45-56.*

Italy's fourth biggest lake, Trasimeno, to the west of Perugia, is a shallow saucer of water surrounded by low hills. Its three wooded islands – Polvese, Maggiore and Minore – were all visited by St Francis and have ancient churches.

The lake retains some of its ancient fishing industry and has long had strategic significance – it was the site of one of the worst military defeats of the Roman Empire, when Hannibal, having led his troops, plus elephants, over the Alps, lured Flaminius's Roman army into an ambush and killed at least 15,000 soldiers.

Trasimeno is fed almost exclusively by rainwater, and there have been occasional plans to drain it, though the current threat is climate change: its level is already much lower than in ancient times, and it is in danger of drying out completely.

Castiglione del Lago is the most attractive lakeside town, with a regular ferry service to Polvese and Maggiore. Set back from the lake to the south, Panicale is a pretty hill town; beyond here, Città delle Pieve was the birthplace of Perugino and still has several of his works. Along the northern edge of the lake the motorway and railway spoil the peace somewhat, though there are some walking opportunities in the hills. A bike path along the water's edge provides some rare flat Umbrian cycling.

Arriving at Lago Trasimeno
Getting around Regular ferry boats leave Castiglione del Lago for Isola Maggiore (eight a day in summer, €6.60 return) and San Feliciano, on the eastern shore, for Isola Polvese (10 a day in summer, €4.80 return). There are fewer boats in winter – check www.umbriamobilita.it. For more luxury, and freedom from the timetable, you could charter your own boat, with the option of strawberries and Prosecco on board, from **Navilagando** ① *T333-570 9373, www.navilagando.com.* Passignano, on the train line at the northern edge of the lake, also has ferries to the islands, but there is less reason to visit the town itself.

Castiglione del Lago
With Etruscan and Roman origins, Castiglione del Lago is an obvious place for habitation, on a high spur jutting out into the shimmering water. Once, long ago, it was an island, but the lake has long since receded to leave the town, with its impressive castle, high and dry.

The town's eponymous fortress, the **Rocca del Leone** ① *T075-951099, hours variable,* €5, was once fought over by Cortona and Perugia. The outside walls are well enough preserved to allow visitors to walk all the way around the ramparts and up a couple of the towers, from where there are great views of the lake past the stentorian signs. The castle keep reopened only in 2008 after sustaining damage in the 1997 earthquake. A ticket to the fortress also gets you into the **Palazzo della Corgna**, connected to the castle by a long fortified passage. The palace, where both Machiavelli and Leonardo da Vinci stayed in their day, is less interesting than the fortress, despite its large military frescoes.

The rest of Castiglione del Lago is a good place to wander, though without too much in the way of must-see sights. The main street is packed with food, wine and ice cream shops, and many of the delicatessens on and around the main piazza give out free tastes of their wares.

Panicale

A pretty little hill town 13 km south of Castiglione del Lago, Panicale has good views to Castiglione del Lago and the distant lake itself. It also has the impressive sloping piazza Umberto I, dominated by the **Chiesa di San Michele Arcangelo**. Built in the 11th century, the church has a baroque interior containing the *Adoration of the Shepherds* (1519) by Gianbattista Caporali, a student of Perugino: €0.05 gets you 21 seconds of light and piped organ music.

Perugino himself is represented in the **Chiesa di San Sebastiano**, where his large fresco of the *Martyrdom of St Sebastian*, painted in 1505, can be seen. A wander along quiet, concentric rings of streets will eventually bring you to the 14th-century **Palazzo del Podestà** at the very top of the town.

About 4 km to the west of Panicale, **Paciano** is another attractive hill village.

Città della Pieve

South of Lake Trasimeno (20 km from Castiglione del Lago) this town was, despite his nickname, the birthplace of Pietro Vannucci (commonly known as Perugino) in 1446. Built mainly in red brick, the handsome medieval buildings have a diffferent feel to the pale stone structures in the rest of the region. Vicolo Baciadonne ('kissing ladies street') is claimed to be one of the narrowest streets in Europe – so much so that amorous contact with anyone coming the other way is almost inevitable. A ticket for the so-called **Museo Diffuso** ① *from the tourist information office in piazza Matteotti, T0578-299375, €4*, covers five sights: the **Cattedrale**, the **Palazzo della Corgna**, the **Oratorio di Santa Maria dei Bianchi**, the **Chiesa di Santa Maria dei Servi** and the **Chiesa di San Pietro**. All except the *palazzo* have Perugino frescoes from the beginning of the 16th century. In the Oratorio di Santa Maria dei Bianchi, Perugino's *Adoration of the Magi* is accompanied by a letter detailing the financial negotiations between the artist and the church.

Isola Polvese

The largest island on the lake, and also the most attractive, Polvese is a nature reserve, carefully protected. The island has 6000 olive trees as well as oak woods, and had a population of around 500 people in medieval times, supported by fishing. Guided tours of the island are available from the **information office** ① *T075-965 9546, www.polvese.it*, near the ferry landing.

The **Fortezza Medievale** dates back to the 13th century, when the lake was an important economic and strategic area and villagers needed protection against attack. In summer it is used for occasional concerts as part of the **Trasimeno Blues Festival** (see page 54).

The **Monasterio di San Secondo** was built by monks who inhabited the island from the end of the 15th century. The island also has a garden of aquatic plants. A good walk follows a path around the edge of the island, taking an hour or so. There is a beach to the northeast of the landing point, from where it is possible to swim.

Isola Maggiore

The most easily reached of the lake's islands, Maggiore also has the most developed tourist infrastructure, with restaurants and shops vying for the trade of visitors the moment they step off the boat. Few visitors make it far from the quayside, however, leaving most of the island a rewarding place to explore.

Paths climb to the summit, where there are 360° views and the 13th-century **Chiesa di San Michele Archangelo** ① *daily 1000-1300, 1400-1745, combined ticket with Lace*

Museum €3. Frescoes here were painted between the 13th and 16th centuries and include a *Madonna and Child* from 1280. The four spandrels above the altar depict the four evangelists.

Another path around to the north of the island skirts the edge of the water, leading to places where you can swim, though if you're put off by the idea of lukewarm green murk it may not be for you. Also here is a shrine to St Francis, who spent time on the island. Higher up the hill you can visit the cave where he is supposed to have slept.

Nearby **Isola Minore** is privately owned and can't be visited.

Perugia, Assisi and Lago Trasimeno listings

For hotel and restaurant price codes and other relevant information, see pages 11-15.

🛏 Where to stay

Perugia *p22, map p24*
Many people come to Perugia to study, and there's an unusually good selection of short- to medium-term accommodation available. Prices for an apartment sleeping 2 range from around €500 per month up to about €850. The website www.studentliving.eu has listings.
€€€€ Brufani Palace, piazza Italia 12, T075-573 2541, www.brufanipalace.com. One of the region's smartest hotels, the 5-star deluxe **Brufani** is a large, old-fashioned place, with 94 rooms and a swimming pool with a glass bottom, under which are Etruscan remains. There's an expensive restaurant (€€€) and a stylish bar, all leather and walnut, which is also open to non-residents and has seating outside in the piazza in summer. Rooms are furnished with sumptuous fabrics and all the comforts imaginable.
€€€€ Castello dell'Oscano, strada Forcella 37, Cenerente, T075-584371, www.oscano.com. A 19th-century faux-antique castle set on a wooded hill 7 km north of Perugia, the **Castello dell'Oscano** has a great restaurant and elegant rooms, though it can feel more like staying in a country house than a bona fide castle. There are good views over the peaceful valley from the crenellated rooftop, a small pool, gym and sauna. There are also rooms in the neighbouring **Villa Ada**.

€€€€ Castello di Monterone, strada Montevile 3, T075-572 4214, www.castello monterone.it. Less than 10 mins outside Perugia, on the town's pretty eastern side, this is a castle with neo-Gothic touches but plenty of romance in its 18 rooms. Originally built in the 12th century, the castle was restored in the 1800s and is decorated with pieces such as an Etruscan urn, a 14th-century crucifix and a Roman bust. There's a smart restaurant in the ex-dungeon, an outdoor terrace, a bar with a huge fireplace, and a swimming pool. The beds and other furniture are all handmade in Umbria and the hotel has beehives, vines and olives. If money is no object, book the Camera delle Dame, with frescoes of damsels and windows looking out in 3 directions, from which you can watch the sun setting behind a great vista of Perugia.
€€€ Hotel Fortuna, via Luigi Bonazzi 19, T075-572 2845, www.albergofortuna.it. This greenery-clad building just off piazza della Repubblica has 52 rooms, the best of which have 18th-century ceiling frescoes. Standard rooms are plain but comfortable, with pale fabrics and wooden floors; 'executive' rooms have exercise bikes. There's an antique library and good views from the small roof terrace.
€€€ Il Romitorio di Monte Tezio, località strada Colognola, Migiana di Monte Tezio, T075-690859, www.montetezio.it. Closed Feb. In the peaceful hills of the Monte Tezio park, a 20-min drive north of Perugia, the **Romitorio** is a converted 13th-century monastery, complete with a church and

a vegetarian restaurant built from the old stables. There are 7 bedrooms, plus 2 flats sleeping up to 6 people, all simply but elegantly furnished. The farm has animals, including horses, and riding lessons and treks are offered. Free transfer from Perugia airport.

€€€ **La Rosetta**, piazza Italia 19, T075-572 0841, www.perugiaonline.com/larosetta. Big and central, the old-fashioned **Rosetta** has 18th-century ceiling frescoes in its grandest rooms and badly reproduced paintings elsewhere. 2nd floor rooms are more modern, with good black and white tiled bathrooms. Rooms overlook either the *corso* or a paved internal courtyard.

€€€ **Le Torri di Bagnara**, strada della Bruna 8, Pieve San Quirico, T075-579 3001, www.letorridibagnara.it. This converted 11th-century abbey 22 km north of Perugia has 7 double rooms and suites, and 4 apartments of various sizes in a stone tower. The buildings are part of a large estate with mountain biking routes, woods and lakes. There's a large pool, and great views.

€€ **Anna**, via dei Priori 48, T075-573 6304, www.albergoanna.it. Friendly if occasionally eccentric, **Anna** is run by an elderly couple who know how to look after guests. Rooms are small and breakfast is best avoided, but the position – just a couple of mins down the hill from the *corso* – is great, and you'll soon feel like one of the family. They also own **Hotel Domus**, further down the hill.

€€ **Azienda Agricola Biologica Torre Colombaia**, San Biagio della Valle, T075-878 7381, www.torrecolombaia.it. One of the 1st certified organic farms in Italy, **Colombaia** is a set of converted hunting lodges in 80 ha of woods about 17 km southwest of Perugia. There are 4 more double rooms in the main house, where there's also an organic restaurant. There's good scope for birdwatching, and free yoga lessons in a meditation room.

€€ **Primavera Mini Hotel**, via Vincioli 8, T075-572 1657, www.primaveraminihotel.it. Near piazza Morlacchi, this friendly little family-run hotel is on the 2nd and 3rd floors of a building on a quiet side street. 8 rooms have TV, free Wi-Fi and minibars, and one, at the top, has a private terrace with great views across the Perugian rooftops. The rooms are plain but comfortable, with wooden floors and fairly modern furniture. It's popular, so book ahead.

Assisi *p34, map p36*

€€€ **Castello di Petrata**, via Petrata, T075-815451, www.castellopetrata.com. Though it can sometimes feel a little too large for its own good, **Castello di Petrata** has a great position in the hills behind Assisi, a beautiful pool and other perks such as a billiards room, a restaurant and an open fire. You can hire mountain bikes, and in summer there is cooking outdoors.

€€€ **San Crispino**, via Sant'Agnese 11, T075-815 5124, www.sancrispinoresidence. com. 7 suites down the hill from Santa Chiara all have little kitchens cunningly disguised as dressers, which open out to reveal a fridge and small cooker. The beds are draped with fabric and the biggest room has its own terrace, with sun loungers and fantastic views. There are mod cons too – rooms come with flatscreen TVs and internet-equipped computers. The same people own a 'resort' 5 km outside Assisi with a pool and gym.

€€€ **Subasio**, via Frate Elia 2, T075-812206, www.hotelsubasio.com. Charlie Chaplin and Italian royalty once stayed here, right next to the Basilica di San Francesco. These days the hotel has lost some of its polish, but enough of the early to mid-20th century touches have been preserved to retain some style. Walnut furniture and carpets are the order of the day, and some rooms have small baths and even smaller balconies.

€€ **Agriturismo Alla Madonna del Piatto**, via Petrata 37, Pieve San Nicolò, T075-819 9050, www.incampagna.com. You will be exceptionally well looked after at this beautiful little place high in the hills above Assisi. There's a minimum stay of

2 nights, 3 in high season. Home-made printed guides to local day trips are offered, and there's a good library of guidebooks. A vine-entwined pergola has views across the rolling countryside to the back of the Basilica di San Francesco, as does one of the guest bathrooms. The oldest part of the house dates back to around 1500, when it may have been a watchtower, and 2 rooms downstairs have stone barrel vaulting. Upstairs, slightly more modern rooms are cosy, with underfloor heating, and all are attractively but soberly decorated, with iron-framed beds. Letizia runs cookery lessons every week in season, for both guests and non-guests.

€€ Hotel il Palazzo, via San Francesco 8, T075-816841, www.hotelilpalazzo.it. A friendly place in the centre of Assisi with 12 rooms, all different. There are original 16th-century ceilings with wooden beams, art on the walls, and a cool, private courtyard. The bathrooms are white tiled and spotless. A suite is much bigger, with a frescoed ceiling and the top floor has panoramic views.

€€ Pallotta, via San Rufino 6, T075-812307, www.pallottaassisi.it. A homely little B&B up the hill from piazza del Comune. Terracotta-tiled bedrooms have large reproductions of oil paintings from the gallery down the road, and tiny bathrooms. Upstairs there is a beautiful 'belvedere', with comfy seats and huge windows looking out over Assisi. There's a washing machine, Wi-Fi and even umbrellas that guests can use for free. Guests get a 10% discount in the excellent **Trattoria Pallotta**, across the piazza.

Self-catering
Brigolante Guest Apartments, via Costa di Trex 31, T075-802250, www.brigolante. com. 3 self-catering apartments on a farm in the hills to the north of Assisi, sleeping 2-4 people. Nice touches include handmade soap, a wood-burning fire and a balcony overlooking Monte Subasio. Bedrooms have metal-frame beds and there are kitchen facilities as well as satellite TV. Sometimes available for 2-night stays in low season, €475 a week in high season.

Lago Trasimeno *p43*
€€€€ Villa di Monte Solare, via Montali 7, Colle San Paolo, Panicale, T075-832376, www.villamontesolare.com. One of Umbria's most elegant hotels, the **Villa di Monte Solare** has 25 rooms high in the hills to the south of Lake Trasimeno among olive groves and vines and sweeping views south. There's a formal garden with lemon trees, breakfast comes with cooked eggs and sparkling wine, and there are 2 swimming pools, with great views. The state-of-the-art spa, **Le Muse** (see page 56) is luxurious, and there's a cookery school for guests. From May to Oct classical music concerts are held in the small chapel. Built in 1780, the main building is the most desirable, with painted wooden ceilings and antiques-filled rooms.

€€€ Capricci di Merion, via Pozzo 21, Tuoro sul Trasimeno, T075-825002, www. capriccidimerion.it. A romantic *stile Liberty* house in the peaceful hills to the north of the lake, this square villa was built for Lady Merion by her lover Baron Rondò. Rooms, named after poets, composers and artists, are individually decorated, with plenty of antique character and colour; some have metal-framed 4-poster beds. There is a swimming pool in the gardens, a sunbed and sauna, and the restaurant (see page 53) is excellent.

€€€ Casa Bruciata, locale San Bartolomeo dei Fossi, Preggio, T075-941 0277, www. casabruciata.com. Isolated in the hills to the north of the lake, **Casa Bruciata** is a collection of buildings with apartments sleeping between 2 and 6 people, which can be rented by the night or the week. There's a swimming pool with great views, a restaurant, and lots of home-grown produce that guests usually have access to.

€€€ Il Cantico della Natura, Case Sparse 50, Montesperello di Magione, T075-841699, www.ilcanticodellanatura.it. An ecologically minded place to the east of Lago Trasimeno,

Il **Cantico** has 12 beautifully designed rooms, each named after a month of the year, with dark wooden beams and draped beds. They run a good range of themed weekends 'for those who love' or for those who fancy a trip in a hot-air balloon.

€€ Fattoria Il Poggio, Parco Naturale Isola Polvese, T075-965 9550, www.fattoria isolapolvese.com. The accommodation may be fairly basic, but the opportunity to stay on Isola Polvese and have the island more or less to yourself after the last boats have gone is worth giving up a few luxuries for. There are apartments and rooms, and films, fishing trips, canoeing and yoga courses can all be organized.

€€ Il Torrione, via delle Mura 4, Castiglione del Lago, T075-953236, www.iltorrionetrasimeno.com. One of Lake Trasimeno's best deals, Il Torrione's 2 nicest rooms open on to a geranium-filled garden built right into the top of one of the ancient towers in the town's protective walls. Colourful modern art decorates the walls of the 5 simple, square rooms, which are equipped with fridges. There's also an apartment with a kitchen.

€€ Lillo Tatini, piazza Umberto I 13, Panicale, T075-837771, www.lillotatini.it. A beautiful little medieval apartment in Panicale, owned by the restaurant of the same name. Bare stonework and arches retain the original feel, but there are newer, more personal touches too, such as the coloured tiles around the cooking area. Ask about special weekends such as a wine and food package, where for €160 per person guests get accommodation plus 2 full suppers in the restaurant with wine, plus *aperitivi* in Caffè della Piazza.

€€ Miralago, piazza Mazzini 6, Castiglione del Lago, T075-951157, www.hotelmiralago. com. From the pastel shades to the bronze dog statues, Miralago has a slight 1980s feel. It is, however, plum in the centre of Castiglione del Lago, and most of its 19 light, comfortable rooms overlook the lake or the piazza or both.

❼ Restaurants

Perugia *p22, map p24*

€€€€ Nanà, corso Cavour 202, T075-573 3571. Mon-Sat 1300-1430, 2000 till late. In a large, yellow, high-ceilinged room, Nanà is a smart and serious restaurant with friendly and very efficient service. There are some tasty starters, such as carpaccio with walnuts and celery, the home-made pasta is delicious and the meaty seconds are generous. Try the thali-style cheese and fruit selection, with 10 different cheeses, and leave some room for one of the exceptional home-made desserts, especially the crème caramel ("done properly"). The wine list could be used to prop a door open, but is thin on local wines.

€€€€ Ubu Re, via Baldeschi 8a, T075-573 5461, www.ubure.it. Cosed Sat lunch, all day Sun, Mon eve, 2 weeks in Aug. One of Perugia's most sophisticated restaurants, Ube Re is smart but never stuffy, and has a nice personal, human touch. Delicious tasting menus focus on fish or meat, and there's also a rare vegetarian menu. Dishes are imaginative and full of interesting flavours: try the black lasagne with mussels and saffron, or duck with pistachios and plum sauce. The bread is good too – home-made and with inventive flavourings – and there's a great choice of cheeses, though you should save some room for the peach strudel with cinnamon ice cream and red wine sauce. The friendly staff are very knowledgeable about the extensive wine list. Jazz plays, Paul Klee posters give a touch of contemporary style, and there's even a collection of books to browse should conversation falter.

€€€ Al Mangiar Bene, via della Luna 21, T075-573 1047, www.almangiarbene.com. Mon-Sat 1220-1600, 1930-2300. Down a steep stepped lane from corso Vannucci, Al Mangiar Bene is a warmly welcoming place with an entirely organic wine list and food to match. In an a/c, rib-vaulted space they serve wood-fired pizzas as well as excellent traditional Umbrian food. The vegetarian choices are especially good, and wide-ranging, and even the chocolate mousse is unusually tasty. The mixed antipasti are good and plenty for 2, and for *primo* you can choose a type of pasta and a sauce, or go for the home-made gnocchi, then follow it up with some more expensive meat options.

€€€ Bottega del Vino, via del Sole 1, T075-571 6181, www.labottegadelvino.net. Mon-Sat 1200-1500, 1900-2400, closed Aug. Overlooking piazza Danti, this atmospheric and genial wine bar serves some of Perugia's best food to hip young locals and a smattering of in-the-know tourists. The pasta menu changes daily, and there are some excellent salads. A bicycle hangs from the ceiling, jazz plays (with live performances on Wed), the place is decorated with candles, old photos of Perugia and Umbria Jazz posters, and the staff are knowledgeable and friendly.

€€€ Civico 25, via della Viola 25, T075-571 6376, www.civico25.com. Mon-Sat evenings only, closed Aug. On a quiet back street, this wine bar and restaurant attracts a good mix of genial drunks and smart young Perugians. A bar at the front is a good spot to drop by for a quick glass of wine, while the tight, colourfully modern tables on 2 levels at the back are food-centred. The *degustazione* starter – a mix of whatever the chef fancies giving you – is generous and exceptionally good, and may include tasty delicacies such as a stuffed chilli pepper, a cheese tart and *panzanella* (bread and tomato salad). Service is very professional and you can see into the semi-open kitchen. There are also a few outdoor tables across the road.

€€€ La Lumera, corso Bersaglieri 22, T075-572 6181, www.lalumera.it. Wed-Mon 1900-0100. Just outside porta Pesa, **La Lumera** is a local restaurant with a loyal clientele. Inside are wooden tables, a tiled floor and old photos covering the walls, but in summer it mostly moves outside, with tables haphazardly scattered in an alleyway. The menu features an excellent sardine tart, an unusual variety of bread and a good range of

traditional Umbrian classics, such as *umbricelli* (thick spaghetti) with pecorino cheese. Their support for the Slow Food movement can go too far, however, with service that sometimes moves at a glacial pace.

€€€ La Piazzetta, via Deliziosa 3, T075-573 6012. Wed-Mon 1200-1500, 1900-2300. This is an Umbrian restaurant with a rare international focus. There's a 'creative' menu and a fish menu alongside the more standard choices – try the apricot with marinated salmon and spring onion, or the beef with courgette flowers and truffles. And if you're having trouble choosing, the *antipasti della casa* are a great mix of inventive starters. Service is friendly, multilingual and eager to help, and the restaurant is equally popular with locals and visitors, despite being hidden away on a side street off via dei Priori. 6 tables outside under a pretty vine-covered arbour are 1st choice in summer, but there's also a brick-vaulted interior.

€€€ L'Officina, Borgo XX Giugno 56, T075-572 1699, www.l-officina.net. Mon-Fri lunch and dinner, Sat-Sun evenings only. One of Umbria's most intelligent, metropolitan eateries, sophisticated l'Officina is a cultural centre, mounting excellent contemporary art exhibitions, as well as a wine bar and restaurant. Dishes are not simple, but well thought through, and without fail delicious. The beef tartar antipasto is beautifully presented, with an exquisite rocket pesto, a quail's egg, Parmesan and red onion chutney. Rabbit and tripe feature in some meaty first and second courses, but don't miss out on the wonderful desserts, including a spectacular raspberry soufflé. A glass-fronted kitchen means you can see the performance art of food preparation going on.

€€€ Osteria del Bartolo, via Bartolo 30, T075-571 6027. Thu-Tue evenings only, closed most of Aug. Small, barrel-vaulted and sunk down from the street, eating at **Bartolo** feels like dining in a wine cellar, and the wine list is suitably long, with lots of bottles on display at each end of the room. Chianina beef (bred in the region for centuries) is a speciality – you can have it in a stew or as carpaccio. The 'fright' fish is also excellent: tasty and in a satisfyingly herby batter.

€€€ Osteria del Gufo, via della Viola 18, T075-573 4126, www.osteriailgufo.it. Tue-Sat 2000-0100, closed Aug. On a winding back street, **Gufo** is well worth seeking out for its buzzing atmosphere and great home cooking. Friendly and down to earth, it mixes Umbrian tradition and good, seasonal, local ingredients with a touch of imagination to make just about the perfect *osteria*. There's a good wine list too, though many will be happy with the house wine – fantastic value at €1 a glass. The menu changes regularly but, if they're available, try the delicious *maccheroni* with smoked sausage and the wild boar with fennel. Unusually, the home-made desserts, such as a much-better-than-it-sounds potato and almond pudding, are also very good.

€€€ Trattoria del Borgo, via della Sposa 23a, T075-572 0390, www.trattoriadelborgo. com. Mon-Sat 1930-2400, closed Aug. Just off the bottom of via dei Priori, this popular and friendly place, with white walls and wooden beams, is run by a former butcher and his wife. Everything is home-made, from the excellent pasta to the tasty desserts. In addition to the traditional menu, daily specials make good use of seasonal ingredients. As you might expect, the meat is very good, but there are plenty of vegetarian options too. Arrive early or book ahead.

€€ Dal Mi' Cocco, corso Garibaldi 12, T075-573 2511. Tue-Sun 1300 onwards, 2015 onwards. A simple, traditional and popular place, this offers choice only in the sense that you can choose which day to go on. Tue is rice, Thu gnocchi, but there's always pasta, and the 2nd course is usually mixed grilled meat. €13 gets you very generous portions and side dishes and a dessert too. Wheat sheaves, brick vaulting and old jazz add some style and, as you might expect, it's popular with students,

though it also fills up with Italian families and businessmen.

€€ Il Bacio, via Boncambi 6, T075-572 0909. Daily 1200-1530, 1900-2430. You'll need to allow an hour or so to read through all the pizza choices, which include turnip tops. In summer there are tables outside in the middle of corso Vannucci for the best front row seats in town. Service can be less than attentive, but the good-sized, tasty pizzas and the views are well worth it.

€€ Locanda Do' Pazzi, corso Cavour 128, T075-572 0565, www.locandadopazzi. it. Mon-Sat 1200-1500, 2000-2300. A cosy trattoria decorated with an extraordinary chandelier resembling a sort of upturned Venus flytrap, and lots of clocks, none of which tell the right time, in brick-vaulted rooms on a corner of corso Cavour. **Do' Pazzi** offers bargain lunches, with 2 courses from €9, and tasty fresh home-made pasta, as well as traditional meat dishes such as sausages and broccoli.

€€ Osteria del Tempo Perso, via Piacevole 13, T075-572 9831. Mon-Sat 2030-0300. One of Perugia's best-value restaurants is hidden away near the Università per Stranieri: take the steps to the right off via Piacevole and look for the door under the streetlamp. Slightly self-consciously old-fashioned, it serves wine in pottery cups. Candles and bare stone walls add to the atmosphere, as does the slightly strange mix of ancient Italian pop, jazz and 1970s disco. There is a concise menu of tasty daily specials, or you can book paella in advance.

€€ Pizzeria Etruschetto, corso Garibaldi 17, T075-572 9230. Mon and Wed-Fri 1200-1430, 1800-2330, Sat-Sun 1800-2400. Proper Neapolitan pizza, and a proper Neapolitan atmosphere to boot. Eat in or take away, either in traditional rounds or by the metre. Expect a long wait on Fri or Sat nights if you turn up without a reservation. 2 small rooms are decorated with photos of Naples, and a noisy crowd crams the wooden tables. Drinks are cheap and the pizzas are the some of the best in town.

€€ **Pizzeria Mediterranea**, piazza Piccinino 11/12, T075-572 1322. Wed-Mon 1230 onwards, 1930 onwards. A real pizzeria, selling nothing other than pizzas, **Mediterranea** does the simple things very well, and buzzes for most of the year. There are 2 rooms, with wooden tables, high, barrel-vaulted ceilings and stone walls, and the big pizza oven is a prime feature. There's plenty of choice, with tasty toppings and lots of fresh ingredients, and both the pizzas and the house wine are excellent value.

€€ **Porchetta stand**, piazza Matteotti. Perugia's cheapest lunch is about as near to fast food as you'll get in the *centro storico*. Most mornings, a van will arrive in piazza Matteotti with a stuffed and roasted pig, and pork rolls will then be sold until the pig has all gone, usually by about 1400.

€ **Nadir**, via Benedetto Bonfigli 11, T388-4831430, www.ristorantenadir.it. Daily from 1900. Underneath Cinema Zenith, thoughtfully prepared and mostly organic food, artisan beer and a good selection of wines.

€ **Osteria a Priori**, via dei Priori, 39, T075-572 7098, www.osteriaapriori.it. Wed-Mon 1200-1500, 1900-0000. In a great contemporary, barrel-vaulted space, with simple wooden stools and dark wood floors, **Osteria a Priori** is a delicatessen as well as a restaurant. An exponent of the Slow Food movement it's a good place to buy beans from Trasimeno or Umbrian wines. The food concentrates on simple local fare: pasta made with organic flour, frittata with seasonal truffles and a great selection of cheeses and cold meats. There's an olive oil menu and artisan local beer too.

Cafés and bars

Caffè di Perugia, via Mazzini 10, T075-573 1863, www.caffediperugia.it. Wed-Mon 0730-2400. Though it can't match the bijou stylishness of **Caffè Sandri**, **Caffè di Perugia** is a smart, big, brick-vaulted place in a medieval building that carries off its chandeliers and peach tablecloths with aplomb. There are seats outside, but the cosy interior is especially suited to winter. You can also eat here, or try some local wines in the *enoteca*.

Caffè MedioEvo, corso Vannucci 70, T075-572 4129. Fri-Wed 0800-2400. A place to see and be seen, pricey **MedioEvo** is the pick of the corso Vannucci cafés. Its tables have pride of place on piazza della Repubblica, and there are good pastries for breakfast and decent snacks on wooden boards at *aperitivo* time. If you don't mind missing the Perugian parade on show outside, the interior is beautiful, with decorated arches and subtle green and red walls.

Caffè Sandri, corso Vannucci 32, T075-572 4112. Thu-Tue 0800-2200. There's old-fashioned elegance and style in abundance here, with glass-fronted wooden cabinets and red-jacketed staff. It's worth having a coffee just to stand at the bar and marvel at the frescoed, vaulted ceiling, but you may also be tempted by the home-made sweets.

Cioccolateria Augusta Perusia, via Pinturicchio 2, T075-573 4577, www.cioccolatoaugustaperusia.it. Some of Perugia's best ice cream, and home-made granita – especially good for hot summer afternoons.

Énonè, corso Cavour 61, T075-572 1950, www.enone.it. Wed-Mon 1900-0100. With dark wood, chrome and disco beats, **Énonè** is a funky, modern wine bar, with a ceiling wave lit by halogen lights, a long wine list and more than 25 different grappas. The food is also excellent, with a good range of antipasti and dishes such as fusilli with prawns and courgettes, tuna steak with caper berries and cherry tomatoes, or a meat and cheese 'wallet'. Even the coffee menu has several choices. A Sun brunch buffet from 1100 makes it a great weekend destination.

Frittole Vineria, via Alessi 30, T338-274 6070. Tue-Sun 1830-0230. Whereas other wine bars may be places to be seen, this is a place to drink wine. The atmosphere is amenable and cosy, and the free early evening bar snacks are original and tasty – watch out for the extremely spicy Calabrese paté. The small interior is rib-vaulted and there are nice design touches such as hanging lamps over the bar. Wine racks and old wine boxes line the walls.

Gelateria Gambrinus, via Luigi Bonazzi 3, T075-573 5620. Off piazza della Repubblica, the place to go for your *passeggiata* ice cream. Queues testify to the high regard in which this place is held.

Il Birraio, via delle Prome 18, T075-572 3920, www.ilbirraio.net. Tue-Sun 1930-0230. You walk past the huge vats to enter this microbrewery with a great, relaxed atmosphere and 2 types of its own beer. It's a surprisingly light, open place, with Arabic influences and a playfulness that combines brightly coloured bird boxes, carefully scratched bar stools, sculpture, dried chillies and lots of cushions. 6 international beers on tap augment the homebrew and there's usually sangria on the go too. *Piadine*, generously big *crostone* and fondue fill the gaps if you're peckish, jazz and blues play, and breastfeeding mothers mix with trendy students.

Assisi *p34, map p36*

€€€ La Fortezza, vicolo della Fortezza, T075-812418, www.lafortezzahotel.com. Tue, Sat-Sun 1230-1430, 1930-2130, Mon, Wed, Fri 1930-2130. Grilled duck with wild fennel, rabbit with apple sauce, and guinea fowl with truffles are some of the options at this refined restaurant up stairs from piazza Comune near the centre of Assisi, which has barrel-vaulted brick ceilings and a stuffed boar's head to keep you company.

€€€ La Lanterna,via San Rufino 39, T075-816399. Tue-Sun lunch and dinner. Up a narrow side street off via San Rufino, **La Lanterna** has candlelit tables outside under big white canvas umbrellas. Pizzas, cooked in a real wood-fired oven by a Neapolitan *pizzaiolo*, are excellent, and there's a 3-course pasta and meat menu. Inside it's surprisingly spacious, with white walls and open stonework.

€€€ Medio Evo, via Arco dei Priori 4, T075-813068, www.ristorantemedioevoassisi.it.

Tue-Sun 1230-1500, 1900-2245. A smart, vaulted place down the hill from piazza del Comune, with suited waiters, pristine white tablecloths and low lighting, **Medio Evo** has a high-quality traditional Umbrian menu. There's home-made pasta such as the ubiquitous *strangozzi* with truffles and a good choice of *secondi* such as baked goats' cheese with tomatoes and rosemary, or rabbit cooked in Montefalco wine.

€€€ Trattoria Pallotta, vicolo della Volta Pinta 3, T075-812649, www.pallottaassisi.it. Wed-Mon 1215-1430, 1915-2130. With arches and barrel vaults, this is an elegant but good value restaurant off piazza Comune opposite the Minerva Temple. A mix of in-the-know tourists and locals fill the small tables and are served by exceptionally friendly staff. Unusually for Umbria, there are some excellent choices for vegetarians, with a tasting menu for €24 consisting of 3 courses of inventive dishes. There's plenty of choice for carnivores too, with pigeon and veal featuring strongly among the 2nd course options. Ask for a look in the wine cellar below, which dates back to Roman times.

€€ La Stalla, via Ermeo delle Carceri 8, T075-812317, www.fontemaggio.it. Tue-Sun (daily Jul-Aug) 1230-1430, 1930-2200. In the roughly converted old stalls of a barn 1.5 km east of Assisi, with walls graffitied and blackened by age and smoke, **La Stalla** is a rather unlikely success story, but it has remained almost completely unchanged for decades and is clearly doing something right. Waitresses in red aprons work the meat on an open fire, while pasta and bean dishes appear from the kitchen behind. Try the trademark *bigoli*, made from ricotta and spinach.

Cafés and bars

Caffè del Lion d'Oro, corso Giuseppe Mazzini 11, T075-816420. Daily 0800-2300. A good range of ice creams, including a couple of gluten-free options.

Caffè Duomo, piazza San Rufino 5d, T075-813794. Just up from piazza San Rufino,

Caffè Duomo has round ceramic tables under a giant canvas shade, with jazz and Wi-Fi to go with your *aperitivi*.

Gran Caffè, corso Giuseppe Mazzini 16a, T075-815 5144. Summer daily 0800-2300, winter daily 0800-2000. Few people manage to walk past the spectacular window display of biscuits and pastries – surely Assisi's most photographed – without at least a glance. Inside, its grandness is done in a cartoon fashion, but it's worth putting up with for the cakes.

Lago Trasimeno *p43*

€€€ Country House Montali, via Montali, 23, Tavernelle di Panicale, T075-835 0680, www.montalionline.com. Apr-Nov, dinner served at 2000, reservations required. One of Umbria's few vegetarian restaurants is in a secluded spot high in the hills to the south of Lake Trasimeno. They take their cuisine very seriously here – this is most certainly not a brown bread and sandals sort of place, but rather a smart restaurant and hotel, which has just launched its own cookery book and also runs cookery classes. Try the saffron risotto, or the aubergine tart with a caper and parsley sauce. Strangely, vegans pay 20% more. Should you wish to stay, there are also 10 guest rooms, a pool, and great views.

€€€ Da Sauro, via Guglielmi 1, Isola Maggiore, T075-826168. Daily 1200-1500, closed Nov-Feb. The island's most popular restaurant, at the left-hand end of the main street coming off the boat, **Da Sauro** has a beautiful shaded garden, but struggles to cope when it gets busy. Dishes include tagliolini pasta with smoked tench and other lake fish. Phone ahead or run from the ferry. If it's full, **Ristorante l'Oso** (T075-825 4255), at the other end of the street, is a good alternative. **Da Sauro** also has some rooms to rent.

€€€ I Capricci di Merion, via Pozzo 21, Tuoro sul Trasimeno, T075-825002, www.capriccidimerion.it. Daily, lunch and dinner. If the weather is good, the best seats at **Capricci di Merion** are under the lime trees

in the garden, with views down to the lake. Inside, live harp music accompanies meals. The food is Umbrian with a twist – the 'fantasia', for example, features chocolate gnocchi. Pork is served with grilled fennel and all the dishes are artfully presented.

€€€ La Cantina, via Emanuele 93, Castiglione del Lago, T075-965 2463, www.castiglionedellago.eu/cantina. Daily 1200-1500, 1900-0100. Despite its huge vaulted interior, most people choose to eat in **La Cantina**'s little garden courtyard, complete with views down to the lake. The food is a draw too – tasty dishes such as roulade of trout and rice pudding with saffron and peach sauce are beautifully presented, and there's a very good-value lunch menu, complete with wine and water, for €13. Don't miss the toilets, which you enter through a giant barrel.

€€€ Lillo Tatini, piazza Umberto I 13, Panicale, T075-837771, www.lillotatini.it. Tue-Sun 1230 onwards, 1930 onwards. At the top of the piazza in Panicale, the tables in front of **Lillo Tatini** have great views of everything going on below. The food is imaginative Umbrian, with dishes such as ravioli with quails' eggs and ricotta, smoked tench with rocket, or cannelloni with lake fish, broccoli and lentils.

€€€ Vinolento, via Vittorio Emanuele 112, Castiglione del Lago, T075-952 5262, www.vinolento.it. Tue-Sun 1230-1430, 1900-0100, closed 2 weeks in Nov and 2 weeks in Jan. Castiglione del Lago's most sophisticated eatery offers daily specials such as duck breast with gorgonzola sauce or *taglierini* (thin noodles) with spinach and goose egg. There are tables set back off the main street in summer, or a cosier set up, with small square wooden tables, inside.

Cafés and bars

Caffè della Piazza, piazza Umberto I 13, Panicale, T347-994 2530. Tue-Sun 1000-2000. On Panicale's piazza, this hip little café has an enormous menu of speciality coffees and teas, as well as cocktails and *aperitivi*.

⏏ Entertainment

Perugia *p22, map p24*
Cinema
Teatro del Pavone, piazza della Repubblica 67, T075-572 4911, www.teatrodelpavone. it. English language films Mon, usually at 1800 and 2100, €4. Umbria and Marche have many fine old theatres, often with private boxes and ornate detailing, but few are as accessible as Perugia's most central cinema, in a stunning old theatre right on corso Vannucci. Grab an ice cream from **Gelateria Gambrinus**, a couple of doors down, or microwave some popcorn in the machine in the foyer and choose your own box for a Mon night showing of an English language film.

Clubs
Domus, via del Naspo 3. Tue-Sun 2300-0500. Near piazza Morlacchi, this is the only nightclub in the centre of Perugia. An intimate, brick-vaulted place, popular with students, it has 2 bars and a small dance floor.
Loop Café, via della Viola 19. Daily 0800-0200. Effortlessly hip and Perugia's best spot for live music, **Loop** is also a friendly, cosy and alternative bar, frequented mostly by young Italians who haven't been dressed by their mothers. The music, in a room at the back, is an international and eclectic mix – from a Nirvana tribute band one night to electronica or gypsy folk the next. Gigs on Fri and Sat evenings and often Wed and Thu too. In the daytime **Loop** doubles as a student-friendly café with added art.
Lunabar Ferrari, via Scura 6, T075-572 2966. Daily 0800-0200. Despite the corny name, this is a hip cosmopolitan cocktail bar, with DJs playing sets after 2300. Oversized lamps hang over the red-lit bar and there are several rooms for chilling with a young Perugian crowd. Watch out for the rocking chairs.

Lago Trasimeno *p43*
Music
Panicale, T075-837 9531, www.panicale turismo.it. Has a good calendar of baroque and classical music in its theatre and churches.
Trasimeno Blues, www.trasimenoblues.it. A week-long programme at the end of Jul features international blues artists performing in various locations around the lake.

⏏ Shopping

Perugia *p22, map p24*
Art and antiques
Mario Cardinali – Rigattiere, via della Viola 10, T075-572 4639. Hours vary. A junk shop of the finest order, Mario has a wonderful treasure trove of everything that the residents of Perugia don't want. If you're looking for a battered old cuddly reindeer, an infrared receipt printer or a stylish 1930s clock, this is the place for you. Ask to see the photo of Mario in 1961, when he was a scooter champion.

Books
Feltrinelli, corso Vannucci 78/82, T075-572 6485, www.lafeltrinelli.it. Mon-Sat 1000-2000, Sun 1000-1330, 1600-2000. Perugia's best bookshop is right in the centre of the *centro storico*, perfectly placed for a/c browsing. There are some English-language books, CDs and a decent range of guidebooks among the 40,000 titles.

Clothing
Le Cose di Rita, via della Viola, T340-493 6889. Mon-Fri 1600-2000, Sat 1030-1300, 1630-2000. Well-chosen and attractively displayed vintage clothes at knockdown prices.

Food and drink
Eredi Bavicchi, via dei Priori 15, T075-572 2633. Fri-Wed 0900-1300, 1600-2000, Thu 0900-1300. Many leave Perugia with Perugino Baci chocolates, but much better options are available at

this mouth-watering little shop, which has a fine range of artisan, handmade chocolate, alongside other local specialities.

Markets

Mercato Biologico, piazza Piccinino. 1st Sun morning of each month. Perugia's monthly organic market has a good range of local fruit and veg, as well as cheese, artisan bread and a few stalls of crafts and handicrafts.
Mercato Coperto, off piazza Matteotti. Daily. What is now piazza Matteotti was once the location for Perugia's market, but a new, purpose-built, 3-level covered market has now been constructed outside it. The stalls at piazza level sell bags and shoes – you have to descend to the 2 lower levels to find meat, fish, fruit and vegetables, usually locally grown, high quality and economical.

Photographic supplies

Foto Ottica Fratticcioli, piazza Italia 10, T075-572 6126. A proper photography shop, not a peddler of film and tourist tat, this has an excellent stock of cameras, lenses and equipment plus a wide range of spare batteries and chargers, and friendly staff who know their stuff.

Assisi *p34, map p36*
Art and antiques

Artestampa, via San Francesco 10c, T075-815115. Daily 0930-1300, 1530-1930. Several cuts above your average print shop, Gastone Vignati works here in the back of his shop, where you can see the presses on which he prints lino- and woodcuts of Assisi.

Clothing

Brunelli Felicetti, via Arnaldo Fortini 18, T075-816039. Mon-Sat 0930-1330, 1530-1930, also Sun from 1030, Easter-Oct and Dec. Once upon a time, all Assisi's shops were like this – rough wooden floors, a large counter at the back, goods piled at the sides. The owner of this excellent shoe shop will tell you that the only change since 1922 has been to replace the original light

fitting. And that they're planning to change it back. Aside from nostalgia, they offer a fine selection of shoes, especially sandals.

Food and drink

Alimentari, via San Rufino, T075-816154. Bread, cheese and ham and just about everything you might need for a picnic.

Souvenirs

Arte Legno, via Arnaldo Fortini 20, T075-815 5219, www.artelegnospello.com. Daily, summer 1000-2000, winter 1000-1900. Most souvenir shops around Umbria have a few olive wood chopping boards, but **Arte Legno** has nothing that isn't made out of the intricately veined wood, from wooden spoons to chess sets, including some beautiful pieces.

❶ What to do

Perugia *p22, map p24*
Language courses

Perugia is a popular place to come to learn Italian. The Università per Stranieri means that the infrastructure is good – it's not too hard to find a flat, and there are plenty of others to learn with. The university doesn't do courses less than a month long, however.
Comitato Linguistico, 3rd floor, largo Cacciatori delle Alpi 5, T075-572 1471, www.comitatolinguistico.com. Corner of piazza Partigiani, between Banca dell'Umbria and Infotourist point. Courses for all levels, minimum 2 weeks, €356.
Lingua in Corso, via del Persico 9, T075-374 5044, www.linguaincorso.com. Near the north end of corso Cavour. 1-week courses from €143 for 20 hrs, or €209 for 30 hrs of tuition.
Università per Stranieri, piazza Fortebraccio 4, T075-57461, www.unistrapg.it. Founded in 1921, when Mussolini wanted to spread Italian culture around the world, Perugia's university for foreigners is now cemented as an important part of the city and teaches language and Italian cultural courses to 7500 students from around the world every year.

Month-long intensive Italian courses run during the summer, €400.

Running

Athletics track, Santa Giuliana, via Orsini, near piazza Partigiana. Perugia has few good running routes – roads out of town are mostly steep and lack much in the way of pavements – but the athletics track is open to all for €1.50.

Assisi *p34, map p36*
Language courses

Accademia Lingua Italiana, via Tiberio d'Assisi 10, T075-815281, www.aliassisi.it. Group courses and intensive courses in Italian, including library access, walks and a programme of social events.

Lago Trasimeno *p43*
Cycling

There is a 24-km cycle path around the lake, currently from Castiglione del Lago to Torricella, though it may be extended in future.
Cicli Valentini, via Firenze 68b, Castiglione del Lago, T075-951663, www.ciclivalentini.it. Mon-Sat 0900-1300, 1600-2000. Rents bikes.

Food and wine

Lago Trasimeno vineyards, there are several Colli del Trasimeno wine routes that can be driven, cycled or walked around to visit the lake's vineyards and wine cellars. Contact the **Associazione Strada del Vino Colli del Trasimeno**, T075-847411, www.stradadelvinotrasimeno.it, for maps and further details.

Kitesurfing

Trasimeno's warm, still waters make it a good spot for kitesurfing.
Scuola Kitesurf, Lido di Tuoro, T346-798 2249, www.scuolakitesurf.it. Lessons are available.

Sailing

Club Velico Castiglionese, via Brigata Garibaldi 48, T075-953035, www.cv castiglionese.it. Sailing lessons on the lake.

Walking

Tourist information offices around the lake have maps and suggested walks by the lakeside and in the surrounding hills.

Well-being

Le Muse, Villa di Monte Solare, via Montali 7, Colle San Paolo, Panicale, T075-835 5818, www.villamontesolare.com. Daily 0900-1900. High in the hills to the south of Lake Trasimeno, the location of **Le Muse** spa and beauty centre has a peaceful and relaxing effect before you walk in the door: it's set in the villa's garden in an old *limonaia*, where lemon trees were once kept in winter. Inside are 8 beautifully designed rooms, smiling staff and some great treatments that combine the latest products and trends with Umbrian traditions, such as full-body massages with honey or chocolate. Check the website for good deals that combine spa treatments with meals and accommodation in the **Villa di Monte Solare** hotel (see page 47).

Directory

Perugia *p22, map p24*
Hospital Azienda Ospedaliera di Perugia, via Enrico dal Pozzo, T075-578 2861.
Pharmacy Farmacia San Martino, piazza Matteotti 26, T075-34024, 24-hr service.

Assisi *p34, map p36*
Hospital Ospedale di Assisi, T0758-139227, 1 km southeast of Porta Nuova.
Pharmacy Antica farmacia dei Caldari, piazza del Comune 44, T0758-12552.

Contents

Footprint features

Southern Umbria

Valle Umbra and southeast Umbria

Almost all of Umbria is hilly, which explains the strategic and historical importance of its only sizeable area of flat land – the Valle Umbra, stretching south from Assisi. Once a lake, it is now fertile land, and around its edges is an extraordinary wealth of beautiful walled medieval towns, most built on Roman foundations and little altered for hundreds of years. All repay exploration, with narrow and often cobbled streets leading to ancient churches and sleepy piazzas. The focal point of the area, Spoleto itself, has a prestigious classical music festival as well as some great contemporary art, and in the surrounding countryside there are other attractions – Roman remains, ancient springs, abbeys and waterfalls.

Arriving in the Valle Umbra

Spello is on the same train line as Assisi, and there are also four to six buses daily from Assisi and the same number from Perugia. Trains from Rome on the main line to Ancona call at Foligno (about 90 minutes), and also at Spoleto and Trevi. For stations beyond Foligno towards Perugia, it's often necessary to change.

Spello → For listings, see pages 76-86.

Like Assisi, Spello is a medieval hill town sitting under Monte Subasio, but with the advantage that it has views both over the Valle Umbra and, to the east, over much quieter, more bucolic rolling countryside. There are Roman arches, quiet winding streets, walks up the mountain (and, for the enthusiastic, all the way to Assisi), some stunning Pinturicchio frescoes, and lots of great eating and drinking possibilities.

Most of Spello's sights are near to the main north–south route through the town: from Porta Montanara in the north to Porta Consolare in the south, along via Giulia and via Cavour. Unusually for an Umbrian town, the cobbled streets of the old centre are not closed to traffic, so you'll need to dodge some cars and mopeds. The central piazza della Repubblica is the focus of the old town, but an anomalous disappointment as two of its sides are taken up with ugly 20th-century buildings. The rest of the town is more beautiful, criss-crossed with sloping, stone-paved streets and built in the pastel-shaded limestone of Monte Subasio.

Arriving in Spello

Getting there and around Traffic is restricted in the centre: there's a small, free car park outside Porta Montanara, the gate at the north of the town. Buses run from Perugia and Assisi, but the train is usually a faster option. From Spello station (often unstaffed) it is a relatively easy, if uphill, walk into the town.

Tourist information Tourist information office ⓘ *piazza Matteotti 3, T0742-301009, www.comune.spello.pg.it, summer 0930-1230, 1530-1730, winter 0930-1230, 1530-1730.*

Roman arches and amphitheatre

Around town are a number of ancient Roman arches, in various states of decay. The Roman town of Hispellum was an important base – the religious centre of Umbria under Emperor Constantine. The **Porta Consolare** is the main gateway, at the bottom of town, with three Roman statues decorating its exterior. These were added in the 17th century, having been taken from Spello's **amphitheatre**. The **Porta Venere**, west of piazza della Repubblica, is the most impressive, with two pale limestone dodecagonal towers flanking the arch. Also worth a look is the **Arco dei Cappuccini** (also known as the Porta dell'Arce), just below the highest point of Spello – small but with two complete arches. You can make out the grooves cut into the side by the portcullis that would once have been raised and lowered here. Just to the south you can look down on the ruins of the Roman amphitheatre, suitably juxtaposed with a modern running track.

Chiesa di Santa Maria Maggiore

ⓘ *Piazza Matteotti, daily 0830-1900, free.*

Pinturicchio's exquisite frescoes in the **Cappella Baglioni** lift Spello's most famous church from being a hotchpotch of a building, overlaid with baroque extravagance, into something altogether more remarkable. It's hard not to be drawn in to the painter's masterpiece, which is colourful and full of energy and intriguing details. Watched over by four expressive Sybils on the ceiling are depictions of (from left to right) the *Annunciation*, the *Nativity* and the *Dispute with the Doctors*. There is a self-portrait in the far corner of the *Annunciation*; other details to look out for include ships sailing on a distant sea and an obstinate donkey being pulled across a drawbridge.

Chiesa di Sant'Andrea

ⓘ *Via Cavour, daily 0930-1900, free.*

Built in the 13th century, the Church of Sant'Andrea has another Pinturicchio masterpiece, painted in 1507 and 1508, depicting the *Madonna and Child with Saints*: Lorenzo, Francesco, Ludovico, Andrea and, below, a young John the Baptist. Look for the lightswitch to the right, with a request for donations. Pinturicchio's father was a wool carder, and his well-observed interest in textiles and fabrics is obvious. Also in the church is a beautiful but badly lit 1565 painting by Dono Doni, reminiscent of Raphael.

Pinacoteca Civica

ⓘ *Palazzo dei Canonici, piazza Matteotti, T0742-301497, Tue-Sun Apr-Sep 1030-1230, 1530-1800, Oct-Mar 1030-1230, 1530-1730, €2.60.*

Spello's picture gallery, next to Santa Maria Maggiore, has a beautiful wooden *Madonna*, seated and waving, with her baby on her knee, from around 1240. Other highlights include Andrea d'Assisi's 1503 fresco from the Chiesa di San Bernardino, and a 16th-century terracotta *Pietà*, possibly of German origin. A wooden Christ from the early 14th century has movable arms, which allowed the same sculpture to be used as a crucified and a deposed figure. It was discovered in a storeroom in Santa Maria Maggiore in 1974.

Villa Fidelia

ⓘ *Via Flaminia 72, T0742-651726, Jul-Aug daily 1030-1300, 1600-1900, Apr-Jun and Sep Thu-Sun 1030-1300, 1530-1800, Oct-Mar Sat-Sun 1030-1300, 1500-1800, €3, concession €2.* Just outside the town to the north, inside the yellow walls of early 19th-century Villa Fidelia, is the eclectic **Straka-Coppa Collection** of 19th- and 20th-century art and furniture. There are beautiful formal Italian gardens too, built on an ancient Roman site, and the villa sometimes hosts events – in the past Nick Cave and others have played here.

Monte Subasio → *For listings, see pages 76-86.*

Rising high above the Valle Umbra between Spello and Assisi, Monte Subasio is one of Umbria's most easily accessed bits of highland countryside. Within a couple of minutes of leaving Spello's northeast gate, Porta Montanara, you are in the midst of olive groves, with great views over the surrounding countryside and the Valle Umbra. Higher up, beyond deciduous woods, you emerge onto bare hillside, where the only things that interrupt the vast grassy landscape are a few grazing cows and the occasional monk bent earnestly against the slope. In winter the summit is usually snowbound, but in spring it is covered in wild flowers. St Francis used to come up here to meditate, and it's easy to see why – it seems a place detached from the world below.

The walk uphill is fairly hard going, though the woods are beautiful, especially in spring and autumn. It's possible to reach the top of the mountain in a car – the road into the regional park closes after dark, but during the day it's an exhilarating drive up above the tree line. At a certain point the road becomes gravel, but you can keep going all the way up and down the other side to Assisi, where you arrive at the Porta Cappuccini.

Various parking spots along the way also mean that you can drive some of the way up and then leave the car and continue on foot. To do the whole walk (about 20 km, or six hours), you'll need Kompass map 663, or another good map of Subasio. The tourist information office in Spello provides a photocopied map, but it's fairly indistinct.

Leaving Spello through Porta Montanara, the road continues northeast – if you're driving, continue along here for about 4 km before turning left up a steep and winding road, signposted to **Subasio Camping**. For the walk, take the second right, via Bulgarella, towards Collepino, and you will soon come across a board on the left with a map of Monte Subasio detailing cycling and walking routes. Take the straight path up through the olive groves, following waymarked path 50, bending left and then right again after about 1 km and entering the Subasio park just under the peak of Monte Pietrolungo. Keeping the peak on your right you leave the olives behind and cross a rocky part of the hillside before entering oak and beech woods. Branch left when you reach a junction in a clearing. From here the path continues to the **spring of Fonte Bregno** (around three hours) with occasional expansive views through the trees across the Umbrian plain far below. After the spring you emerge from the trees and climb diagonally across the mountain towards the summit.

Subasio is a loaf-shaped mountain, and it's not always clear where the exact summit is – to reach it, branch right off the path towards the radio masts, crossing the road (which is unsurfaced by this point). At the very top is a trig point, and map boards identifying the various mountains on the horizon. Just below here is the place from which paragliders fling themselves off the mountain: if you're lucky you'll see them taking off.

Return to the mountain bike path, which follows the contours around the slope of the hill to **Rifugio Vallonica** (around four hours 30 minutes) and then bend left down a valley towards the **Eremo delle Carceri** ⓘ *T075-812301, www.eremocarceri.it*, a Franciscan hermitage set up by St Francis himself. It is now home to friars and Poor Clares and open to visitors from 0630-1900 in summer, 0630-1800 in winter.

From the hermitage, follow the road to the right (west) for about 1 km before branching off to the left on a rocky path that leads down through woods to Porta Cappuccini at the top of Assisi. Just down the road from Porta Cappuccini is piazza Matteotti, from where you can get a bus to the train station for the return to Spello.

Bevagna → For listings, see pages 76-86.

A rare flat Umbrian town, Bevagna loses no charm through its lack of slopes. Originally Umbrian, then Etruscan, it became the Roman town of Mevania, on the via Flaminia, which reached here in 220 BC. Much of its current structure is medieval, and it has largely intact walls that still enclose almost the whole of the contemporary town. At its centre, piazza Silvestri is a beautiful spot, with two notable Romanesque churches and the Palazzo Consoli, the consul's building, adapted to contain a theatre in the 19th century.

The town's Roman past can be seen in a stunning mosaic, and the structural outline of an amphitheatre is also visible. A summer festival revives medieval trades, and hand paper-making can be seen in action throughout most of the year. Bevagna's position in the middle of wine-growing country means it has good *enoteche*, and the food is also excellent. It remains a quiet, relatively undiscovered town, with plenty of scope for peaceful wandering.

Arriving in Bevagna
Getting around Three or four buses arrive daily from Foligno, the nearest train station. There is free parking just outside the gates at the northern edge of the town.

Tourist information Tourist information office ① *piazza Silvestri, T0742-361667, www.prolocobevagna.it, summer 0930-1300, 1500-1900, winter 0930-1300, 1500-1800.*

Piazza Silvestri
Bevagna's central point has a great ensemble of medieval buidings. **Palazzo dei Consoli**, dating back to 1187, was once the seat of the town magistrate. Following earthquake damage, when the interior of the building was destroyed, the Teatro Francesco Torti (see below) was built inside.

San Silvestro is a beautiful 12th-century Romanesque church built in pale stone, with sturdy convex columns and a raised chancel. Above the door to the right, an engraved stone shows the date of completion of the church – 1195. The column just inside the door on the right was once the foundation for a bell tower above. On the walls down to the light and airy crypt there are some fragments of frescoes.

The **Chiesa di San Michele Arcangelo**, built in the 12th and 13th centuries, dominates the piazza with its square façade, triple frieze arch around the door and big round window. Inside it's less impressive, with more modern elements mixing with the Romanesque columns and arches.

Museo and Mosaico Romano
① *Corso Matteotti 70, T0742-360031, daily Jun-Jul 1030-1300, 1530-1900, Aug 1030-1300, 1500-1930, Apr-May and Sep 1030-1300, 1430-1800, Oct-Mar Tue-Sun 1030-1300, 1430-1700, €3.50 including tour of mosaic and theatre.*
Bevagna's museum and art gallery has a collection of mainly 17th-century art and an archaeological section (closed at the time of writing) that includes some pre-Roman pieces.

Both are overshadowed, however, by the nearby mosaic floor of the one-time frigidarium of the Roman public baths. Visitable only by guided tour from the museum, it features sea monsters, octopuses and lobsters. A ticket for the museum also entitles you to a tour of the **Teatro Francesco Torti** ① *T0742-361667*, a tiny but perfectly formed theatre built in 1886 inside the medieval Palazzo dei Consoli: it has a busy calendar of drama and music.

Circuito culturale dei mestieri medievali
① *www.ilmercatodellegaite.it, Apr-Nov, Tue-Fri 1030-1230, 1600-1800, Sat-Sun 1000-1230, 1600-1830, €3 for all 4 trades, or €1 each.*
During the last week in June, Bevagna's summer festival, the **Mercato delle Gaite**, revolves around the revival of medieval trades, and some of these can also be seen in action during the rest of the year. The highlight is the medieval paper factory on the square, where handmade paper is still made more or less in the way it was at the time when the first copies of Dante's *Inferno* were printed in nearby Foligno. A waterwheel turns a wooden pulping machine and the whole process is enthusiastically explained. Elsewhere in town there is a candlestick maker, a weaver and a painter.

Montefalco → *For listings, see pages 76-86.*

Marketed as the 'balcony of Umbria', medieval Montefalco sits on a hill on the western side of the Valle Umbra. The 360° views advertised may be a little hyperbolic, but there are certainly some spectacular vistas. There is more exaggeration in the signs at the outskirts of Montefalco: 'wine city, oil city', it says, but in fact it's a small place, not much more than a village, though it has produced six saints in its time, and countless bottles of wine. The most respected wine centre in Umbria, the town is surrounded by vineyards growing the Sagrantino grape, and there are plenty of places to sample and buy the tasty red stuff.

The supernumerary Montefalco saints mean that the town has some impressive, and well-frescoed churches, though the best are reserved for Assisi's St Francis, who gave his famous sermon to the birds nearby. The Church of San Francesco is now a part of the town's worthwhile museum, which also exhibits contemporary art, archaeology and some wine paraphernalia.

Arriving in Montefalco
Ask at Montefalco **tourist information office** ① *piazza del Comune 17, T0742-378490, www.stradadelsagrantino.com, daily 0900-1300, 1400-1800,* for maps and information on local vineyards to visit. The office specializes in vineyards and wine tastings, but can also supply other info. Vineyards are usually open 0900-1230, 1500-1800, but ring ahead to check.

Compleso Museale di San Francesco
① *Via Ringhiera Umbra 6, T0742-379598, daily Aug 1030-1300, 1500-1930; Jun-Jul 1030-1300, 1500-1900; Mar-May and Sep-Oct 1030-1300, 1400-1800; Nov-Feb Tue-Sun 1030-1300, 1430-1700, €5.*
Combining the frescoed Church of San Francesco, the town's museum and art gallery and a contemporary art space, San Francesco is Montefalco's one proper sight.

There is no shortage of art in the church, including Perugino's colourful, pastoral *Nativity*, but Benozzo Gozzoli's *Scenes from the Life of St Francis* in the apse steal the show. Gozzoli's rich and intriguing stories were painted in 1452 and are considered to be one of the most important cycles of Renaissance frescoes.

Downstairs, the so-called monks' wine cellar contains various old utensils and equipment for the manufacture of wine, though the opaque translations into English are less than informative. Also here are fragments of engraved stones and pilasters and a handsome first-century AD Roman funeral altar. Finally downstairs, the *spazi espositivi* are three large barrel-vaulted spaces devoted to temporary – and often good – exhibitions of contemporary art.

Upstairs, in the *pinacoteca*, look out for works by local Renaissance artist Francesco Melanzio, including a downcast *Virgin with Six Saints*.

Piazza del Comune

The centre of Montefalco life, and home to some good wine bars and shops, piazza del Comune is dominated by the town hall, the **Palazzo Comunale**, with an arcaded façade. Look out too for the ex-church of **San Filippo Neri**, now a theatre.

Chiesa di Sant'Agostino

① *Via Ringhiera Umbra.*

A church with a cloister built in the 13th century, Sant'Agostino is notable for its enormous permanent nativity scene, and, bizarrely juxtaposed, a macabre collection of three mummified bodies of holy pilgrims. Flick the switch to turn on the nativity lights and to set the windmill turning and the angels flying, before studying the desiccated faces and wizened toes of the church's oldest residents. Beato Pellegrino, the first of the three, had apparently come to worship the other two, Illuminata and Chiara, when he died in the church. It is said that his body did not decay for 100 years. Should three dead bodies not be enough, you can also visit the cadaver of one of the local saints, Chiara of Montefalco, in the nearby church dedicated to her.

Trevi → *For listings, see pages 76-86.*

Perched high above the valley floor, Trevi is in many ways the archetypal medieval Umbrian hill town. Almost entirely closed to traffic, the old centre – enclosed within Roman and medieval walls – is remarkably quiet; during siesta you might think it uninhabited.

Much of the town's magic is to be found wandering up and down the narrow cobbled streets and steps: happening upon fragments of ancient fresco, glimpsing views of the valley below and watching angular shadows move across the walls. There are also some sights – notably the cathedral, a convent converted into a museum complex, a couple of out-of-town churches that contain significant Renaissance frescoes by Perugino and Lo Spagna, and a good contemporary art centre.

Trevi is surrounded by swathes of olive groves, and oil is everywhere in its shops and restaurants. The town is also proud of its 'black' celery, harvested and sold in autumn, though other than its marginally darker green leaves, you may struggle to notice much difference from conventional celery.

Nearby, ancient springs flow out of the ground at Clitunno, a beautiful spot where Roman emperors once held parties; there are good walks and cycle rides in the surrounding countryside.

Arriving in Trevi

Getting to Trevi by public transport can be challenging. The train station is about 4 km from the town centre and there are few buses to get you up the steep hill into the old town. If you're coming by car there's parking around piazza Garibaldi, to the east of the walls.

Complesso Museale San Francesco di Trevi

ⓘ *Largo Don Bosco 14, T0742-381628, Apr-May and Sep Tue-Sun 1030-1300, 1430-1800; Jun-Jul Tue-Sun 1030-1300, 1530-1900; Aug daily 1030-1300, 1500-1930; Oct-Mar Fri-Sun 1030-1300, 1430-1700, €4.*

The ex-convent now contains a complex of museums under one roof. One ticket admits you to the **Museo della Civiltà dell'Olivo** (Museum of Olive Culture), the paintings in the **Pinacoteca** and archaeological finds in the **Antiquarium**, as well as the **Chiesa di San Francesco** itself.

The most extensive and interesting section is the olive oil museum, downstairs. In places it is a strange mix of dense text on the organoleptic qualities of olives and childish interactive trivia quizzes, but it's a well-designed museum, and there is enough of interest to make it worth a visit.

The highlights of the art gallery are works by Perugino, Pinturicchio and Lo Spagna, whose 1522 *Coronation of the Virgin* also features, on the predella, St Francis receiving the stigmata and St Martin sharing his cloak. The church has a frescoed cloister and a beautiful, elaborately decorated 14th-century organ. The archaeological section is less impressive, despite a Roman sarcophagus and the skeletal remains of a seventh-century Umbrian inhabitant.

Cattedrale di Sant'Emiliano

ⓘ *Via della Rocca, daily 0900-1200, 1600-1800, free.*

In the very centre of the town, Trevi's *duomo*, dedicated to local saint, Emiliano, was built in the 12th century and extended in the 15th. The 19th-century rebuilding of the interior left little of beauty, apart from an elaborate stone altar from 1522, on the left of the nave. Just to the right of this, look out too for a framed fragment of original fresco by Melanzio. Opposite, if the door is open, you can enter a small, dim, frescoed space labelled 'Antica Abside'. Walled off by the baroque restoration, it gives a tantalizing glimpse of the original church.

Palazzo Lucarini

ⓘ *Via Beato Placido Riccardi 11, T0742-381021, www.officinedellumbria.it, Tue-Sun 1600-1900, free.*

Opposite the *duomo*, the bare white walls of the Palazzo Lucarini make a good exhibition space for contemporary art. The temporary shows here are often of high quality and make a refreshing change for anyone tiring of a diet of Gothic and Renaissance religious art.

Chiesa della Madonna delle Lacrime

ⓘ *Via Madonna delle Lacrime, 1 km south of Trevi, opening hours vary.*

In 1485, so it is claimed, tears of blood flowed from the eyes of a painted Virgin in a shrine in a wall on this site. A huge church was subsequently built here, completed in 1522 and frescoed by Perugino (*Adoration of the Magi*, 1521, on the right of the nave) and Lo Spagna (*The Carrying of Jesus to the Tomb*, 1520, in the left transept). To get to the church, leave town by the Porta del Cieco or the Porta della Strada Nuova and head downhill through the olive groves.

Chiesa di San Martino

ⓘ *1 km north of Trevi.*

Overlooking the valley, the convent of San Martino has more frescoes by Lo Spagna. Walk along viale Augusto Ciuffelli from piazza Garibaldi for about 10 minutes to reach the church.

Fonti del Clitunno

ⓘ *Via Flaminia 7, località Fonti del Clitunno, T0743-521141, www.fontidelclitunno.com, daily Jan-Feb 1000-1300, 1400-1630; 1 Mar-15 Mar 0900-1300,1400-1800; 16 Mar-31 Mar 0900-1300, 1400-1830; 1 Apr-15 Apr 0900-1930; 16 Apr-30 Apr 0900-2000; May-Aug 0830-2000; 1 Sep-15 Sep 0830-1930; 16 Sep-30 Sep 0900-1930; Oct 0900-1300, 1400-1800; Nov-Dec 1000-1300, 1400-1630, €3, about 8 km south of Trevi, off SS3 to Spoleto.*

The springs of Clitunno have been a well-known beauty spot for centuries, and Roman Emperor Caligula used to come here for parties. Several springs flow out from the rocks and into large, clear pools, where ducks swim among the rippling reflections of the trees. A bar, café and shop have sprung up since Roman times, but it remains a very pretty spot, peaceful despite the traffic on the road.

Tempietto sul Clitunno

ⓘ *Campello sul Clitunno, Apr-Oct 0845-1945, Nov-Mar 0845-1745, €2.*

About 500 m north of the springs, this early Christian temple is well hidden (and badly signposted) off the main road. Turn left off the SS3 and then immediately right. The temple is a further 400 m or so along this road.

A small building set in lush grass above the water that flows down from the springs, the temple was built using ancient Roman pillars and stones and there are disagreements about its age – estimates range from the fourth to the 13th century.

Spoleto → *For listings, see pages 76-86.*

While Perugia swings along to its summer jazz festival, Spoleto has a more sedate, but equally high quality, classical music festival. Which seems fitting for a town with such a refined air, famous for its elegant 14th-century bridge and its *duomo*. Spoleto's arts credentials run deep – not only does it have some great Renaissance art, it has had a long and happy relationship with modern sculpture, and its contemporary art gallery is excellent.

Arriving in Spoleto

Getting around A funicular is under construction from the bottom of town up the hill. The **Spoleto Card** also entitles you to transport in the minibus which tours around the main sights. Spoleto station is about 1 km from the lower town (further from the upper town). A bus connects the station with the upper town.

Tourist information Tourist information office ⓘ *piazza della Libertà 7, T0743-238920, www.visitspoleto.it, www.comune.spoleto.pg.it, Mon-Fri 0830-1330, 1600-1900, Sat-Sun 0930-1230, 1600-1900.* The town's **Spoleto Card**, www.spoletocard.it, is a worthwhile investment if you're going to be around for a day or two – it covers entrance to all the main sights and costs €9.50 for a week.

Cattedrale di Santa Maria Assunta

ⓘ *Piazza del Duomo, T0743-231063, daily Apr-Oct 0830-1230, 1530-1900, Nov-Mar 0830-1230, 1530-1900, free.*

The beautiful façade of Spoleto's *duomo*, which forms the backdrop to the finale of the Spoleto festival, has eight rose windows and a newer Renaissance portico. The cathedral was built in the 12th century; the portico was added in 1491. The long piazza makes a fine concert venue, as well as a marvellous approach. Inside, there are some great works of art: Fra Filippo Lippi's frescoes of the *Life of the Virgin* on the wall behind the altar are spectacular, and there's an excellent Pinturicchio *Madonna and Child* in the Cappella Eroli. There's also some impressive intarsia (inlaid wood) work in the side chapel at the end on the right, and a beautiful ancient marble floor. Look too for a letter from St Francis in a chapel on the left-hand aisle.

Filippo Lippi, one of the great Renaissance artists, died in 1469 in Spoleto, and the frescoes in the apse of the *duomo* were his last work. Stories abound that he was poisoned – there seems little evidence for this, though he did make enemies during his life. He was buried in the south transept. In the scene of the *Transition of the Virgin* in the centre of the cycle, the man in a white monk's habit and black hat is Lippo Lippi himself – the angel in front of him is his son Filippino, who would become a famous painter.

Rocca Albornoziana

ⓘ *Piazza Campello, T0743-223055, www.sistemamuseo.it; Rocca: Jul-15 Sep Mon 1000-2000, Tue-Sun 0900-2000, Apr-14 Jul and 16 Sep-31 Oct Mon 1000-1800, Tue-Wed and Sun 0900-1800, Thu-Sat 0900-1930, Nov-Mar Tue-Wed and Sun 0900-1700, Thu-Sat 0900-1745; Museo Nazionale del Ducato di Spoleto: Apr-Oct Tue-Wed and Sun 0900-1330, Thu-Sat 0900-1930, Nov-Mar Tue-Wed and Sun 0900-1330, Thu-Sat 0900-1930; €7.50, concession €6.50.*

High above the town and one of the most impressive of the Albornoz fortresses that dot the hilltops of the Valle Umbra – built to exert papal control in the 14th century – Spoleto's

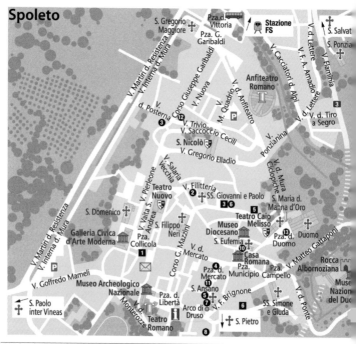

castle has been undergoing restoration ever since it ceased to be a prison in 1982. Mehmet Ali Ağca, the would-be assassin of Pope John Paul II in 1981, was held here.

These days it is home to the **Museo Nazionale del Ducato di Spoleto**. The museum has early Christian and monastic exhibits and some rare artefacts from the Duchy of Spoleto in the sixth, seventh and eighth centuries. A beautifully carved Romanesque stone panel, in which two angels emerge from what were once ancient Roman columns, is among the highlights of the Romanesque and Gothic section. The influence of Giotto is visible in the Piccolomini Apartment, which contains Gothic paintings and sculpture and Renaissance art that was once held in Spoleto's now defunct *pinacoteca*.

When the *rocca* is open but the museum closed, visitors can access the **Cortile d'Onore** and the **Camera Pinta**, decorated with early 15th-century frescoes telling a tale of a rather sad-looking knight.

Ponte delle Torri

The 'Bridge of Towers', 250 m across and, at its highest point, 80 m tall, is Spoleto's must-see sight, and one of Italy's engineering wonders. Built as an aqueduct in the 14th century, possibly on Roman foundations, the bridge is a short walk east of town, just beyond the Rocca. It has spectacular views down into the wooded valley below and across to the Basilica di San Pietro, and makes a great entry point to the excellent network of paths and trails that wind through the woods around **Monteluco**.

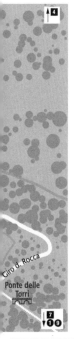

N

| 100 metres |
| 100 yards |

Where to stay 🛏
Charleston **1**
Gattapone **2**
Il Panciolle **3**
Le Terre di Poreta **4**
Palazzo Dragoni **5**
Palazzo Leti **6**
San Pietro in Valle **7**

Restaurants 🍴
Al Cantico **1**
Cantina de' Corvi **2**
Emporio **3**
Gelateria Primavera **4**
Il Mio Vinaio **5**
Il Panciolle **6**
Il Tempio del Gusto **7**
L'Angolo Antico **8**
Osteria Baciafemmine **9**
Osteria dell'Enoteca **10**
Osteria del Matto **11**
Osteria del Trivio **12**
Tric Trac **13**

Basilica di San Pietro

ⓘ *Strade Statale Flaminia 3, T0743-49796, daily 1000-1200, 1530-1700, free.*

A 15-minute walk down from the far side of Ponte delle Torri, or around 10 minutes from piazza della Libertà, the grand but isolated church of San Pietro has a fascinating storyboard of a façade, covered in 12th-century Romanesque bas relief. Grizzly highlights include a man dying a horrible death, helped on by two devils and abandoned by the Archangel Michael, second down on the left. Above, a presumably more righteous person passes away more pleasantly. There are various lions coming face-to-face with humans – and, in some cases, eating them – and there are illustrations of fables involving foxes, wolves, crows and dragons. It's a rich mix of legend and religion, and quite a contrast to the rather dull interior.

Museo Archeologico e Teatro Romano

ⓘ *Via Sant'Agata, T0743-223277, Mon-Sat 0830-1930, €4.*

The Roman theatre is still used for performances, especially during the

Spoleto Festival (see page 16). Dating from the first century AD and excavated from 1954-1960, it is 70 m in diameter. The first two steps, at the bottom of the theatre, are lower and wider and were probably reserved for Roman VIPs.

Alongside the theatre, a well laid out and displayed archaeological museum has two engraved Roman stones forbidding the cutting down of trees in the holy woods of Monteluco, just outside Spoleto. Other highlights include a sensuous but headless female Roman statue revealing one breast, Emperor Augustus's marble head (with a missing nose) and some beautiful eighth-century BC bronze jewellery.

Casa Romana
ⓘ *Via di Visiale, T0743-234250, Apr-Sep Wed-Mon 1100-1900, Oct-Mar Wed-Mon 1100-1700, €3.*
Built just above the ancient forum, where piazza Mercato stands today, a passage leads underground into what must have once been an important Roman house. Indeed it just might have belonged to Vespasia Polla, mother of Emperor Vespasian. A central courtyard has an *impluvium* – a basin for collecting water, which feeds into a cistern. Around this are seven rooms, all with beautiful black and white Roman mosaics in geometric patterns.

Arco di Druso
ⓘ *Via Arco di Druso.*
Just off the piazza del Mercato, the Roman arch was built in AD 23 to mark the military victories of Drusus, son of Tiberius. Drusus was set to become emperor but died at the age of 36, probably poisoned by his wife and an accomplice.

Next to the arch are some stones signposted as a temple – for a better view of its remnants, go down into the medieval **Cripta di Sant'Isacco** under the **Chiesa di Sant'Ansano** ⓘ *daily, 0730-1200, 1500-1830, free*, next door, where St Isaac's carved stone sarcophagus is also well worth a look.

Galleria Civica d'Arte Moderna
ⓘ *Palazzo Collicola, piazza Collicola, T0743-46434, Wed-Mon 16 Mar-14 Oct 1030-1300, 1530-1900, 15 Oct-15 Mar 1030-1300, 1500-1730, €4, concession €1.50.*
In 1962 Spoleto held a sculpture festival, for which 104 pieces of contemporary sculpture were placed around the town. Some are still there, for example at the top of piazza del Duomo and outside the train station. The festival cemented a link between the town and contemporary art, and this museum, which opened in 2000, is one of the best in the region.

Alexander Calder's mobiles set the tone – colourful and playful, they compel the viewer to blow at them. Fifteen rooms of sculpture and paintings include work by Henry Moore, Pietro Ruggeri and a group of local artists, including Leoncillo, whose twisted, melting Roman column is memorable, and de Gregorio, whose thick, heavily brush-marked canvases draw you in. Pino Pascali's lighthearted *Coda di Cetaceo* (whale's tail) won first prize in the 1966 festival, and Sol Lewitt's *Bands of Colour*, painted in 2000, fills an entire room with bright stripes.

Museo Diocesano and Basilica di Sant'Eufemia
ⓘ *Via Aurelio Saffi, T0743-231022, Aug daily 1000-1800; mid-Mar to Jul and Sep-Oct Mon-Fri 1000-1300, 1500-1800, Sat-Sun 1000-1800; Nov to mid-Mar Tue-Fri 1030-1300, 1500-1730, Sat-Sun 1100-1700, €3, children €2.50, concession €3.*
A small picture gallery, Spoleto's diocesan museum has some good religious paintings, such as Filippino Lippi's *Madonna and Child with Sts Montano and Bartolomeo* from

Walks in the hills

To the east of Spoleto a network of paths criss-crosses through the hills, thickly wooded with holm oak. The tourist information office in piazza Libertà has some basic free maps and guides.

To reach the paths, cross the Ponte delle Torri, turn right and go up the steps beside the tower. You may have to duck through the broken fence of a slow-going-on-abandoned restoration project, but after that the trails are well marked and well maintained. The path left from here heads past the outskirts of Spoleto, with good views back to the bridge and Rocca, before turning right up a beautifully peaceful wooded valley.

For mountain bikers there are tougher tracks up and down through the trees and for those in need of a little more exercise, the first couple of kilometres have exercise frames beside the main path.

1485. Look for the tiny picture underneath that shows a bear helping to pull a plough, having killed one of the oxen – a story from the life of St Montano. Andrea da Caldaroa's *Annunciation* (1543) has echoes of Pinturicchio in its botanical detail.

The real star of the show, however, is the Church of Sant'Eufemia, one of the region's most beautiful Romanesque buildings, built in the 12th century and open only to visitors of the museum. You enter halfway up the church, on an unusual raised gallery that runs around three sides and was once reserved for women. A couple of the columns have faded frescoes, but for the most part it is bare, making it easier to appreciate the light, elevated structure of the church.

Basilica di San Salvatore

① *Piazza Mario Salmi 1, T0743-49606, May-Aug 0700-1900, Mar-Apr and Sep-Oct 0700-1800, Nov-Feb 0700-1700, free.*

Outside Spoleto, at the bottom of the hill, is this weird and wonderful Romanesque church. It was built in the fourth and fifth centuries, primarily using Roman remains, and the higgledy-piggledy interior looks as if someone threw the Roman Empire up in the air and sat back to see how it landed.

Pieces of carved stone are built into the walls, upside-down Roman columns are haphazardly patched together and, somehow, the whole thing doesn't fall down. The sun streams in on the pale stone structure, bare and strangely beautiful.

The lower Valnerina → *For listings, see pages 76-86.*

Across Spoleto's spectacular 14th-century bridge, the Ponte delle Torri, to the east of the town, wooded hills and the lower reaches of the Valnerina are an area of semi-wilderness, with a spectacular ancient abbey and where waterfalls created by the Romans are now turned on and off at the flick of a switch. River walks and a museum of mummies are other attractions in the area.

Cascata delle Marmore

① *16 km south of Spoleto on SS3, T0744-62982, www.marmore.it, waterfalls in action all year round, operating more frequently throughout summer, check the website for comprehensive details, €8, concession €5.*

Best of the rest

Umbria has so many attractive towns, so much rolling countryside, that there are many places that couldn't be fitted into this book. Here are just a few tasters:

Foligno Bombed in the Second World War and much maligned since, Foligno is these days mostly known as a railway junction, but there are a few reasons you might want to stop for a little longer. Il Bacco Felice is a popular little restaurant, and there are villas to see and art to peruse.

Terni Umbria's second city, Terni is an ugly, industrial place, especially in contrast to the beauty that surrounds it. It has a few claims to fame though – the gun that shot JFK was made here, and St Valentine was born here. More recently it was used to shoot the concentration camp scenes in *Life is Beautiful*, which just about sums up its contemporary appeal. It does, however, have a good art gallery and an Easter music festival.

Monti Martani Between the E45 and the N3, to the south of Perugia, this sleepy area of hills is little visited, despite its wealth of hill towns and villages.

The Marmore waterfalls, in the lower Valnerina, have a total drop of 165 m, making them among the highest in Europe. Originally created by the Romans, when they diverted the River Velino into the River Nera in 271 BC, the falls are now controlled by the Galleto hydroelectric plant upstream, and water is released according to a complex schedule.

It's a popular destination – especially on summer weekends, when the crowds can make the whole experience feel like an entertainment theme park. However, if you can manage to avoid the worst of the scrums, the falls are a spectacular sight, especially in the late afternoon as the sun streams down through the clouds of spray thrown up by the thundering water.

Chiesa di San Pietro in Valle

ⓘ *22 km southeast of Spoleto, off SS209, look for 1 of 2 turnings to the right just before Colleponte, www.sanpietroinvalle.com, daily 1000-1600 but hours may change, free.*

In a serenely peaceful spot in the Valnerina, high above the valley floor, little has changed in the landscape that surrounds this abbey, and it seems somehow right that so much inside has also survived almost unchanged for so long. A restaurant and sympathetically run hotel (see page 78) have done little to detract from the magic of the place.

At the end of a cypress-lined drive, the abbey nestles in a bend in the hills. From the front, follow the path around to the right to reach the entrance to the church. There has been a place of worship here since at least Roman times, and inside the door to the right is a small conical altar from the first century BC. Other Roman remnants are exhibited on the walls, and the eighth century Faroaldo, Duke of Spoleto and founder of the abbey, is buried in a Roman sarcophagus to the right of the altar, one of six ancient sarcophagi in the church. Most of the structure is Lombard, from the eighth century, or Romanesque, from the 12th century. The church and abbey were restored in the early 20th century, and inaugurated by Mussolini in 1931.

The church has one aisle ending in a three-bay apse, and is richly frescoed with ancient paintings. The 12th-century frescoes on both side walls depict Biblical scenes: the Old Testament is illustrated on the left wall, scenes from the New Testament on the right.

The frescoes, by an anonymous Umbrian artist, are not complete, but all the same they demonstrate a remarkable sense of movement and expression, way ahead of their time. They predate Giotto by around 150 years, and compared to the flat, front-on Byzantine images that were the norm in the 12th century, they must once have seemed very modern. Highlights include Eve being born from Adam's rib, high up on the left side, and Noah receiving news of the flood.

The eighth-century altar is also well worth a look, with its geometric patterns and primitive figures, one of which has the sculptor's signature ('Ursus') on either side of his head.

The cloister is a pretty, two-tier, geranium-punctuated construction, which is now used by the hotel. Look for the statues of St Peter and St Paul on either side of the door.

Opposite the abbey is the ruined **Rocca di Umbriano**, which once looked over the valley and protected the abbey from invaders. From the abbey to Umbriano is about an hour's walk, or you can walk up the steep hill above the abbey (follow the red and white waymarked path just to the south of the building) for some good views of the valley.

Ferentillo

The small town of Ferentillo, 26 km south of Spoleto on SS209, is a climbing centre because of the sheer rock faces across the valley. It also has a weird museum of mummies.

Other villages in the lower Valnerina worth exploring include **Scheggino** and **Arrone**, both of which have narrow, steep streets winding up to views of the valley below.

Museo delle Mummie ① *Chiesa di Santo Stefano, Ferentillo, T0743-54395, Apr-Sep 0930-1230, 1430-1930, Mar and Oct 0930-1230, 1430-1800, Nov-Feb 1000-1230, 1430-1700, closed Sun morning during Mass, €3.* When a new church was constructed in 1500, part of the previous building, put up 300 years earlier, was left underneath as foundations. It served for a long time as the town's cemetery and, by a weird quirk of fate, the bodies that ended up there have been preserved, due to a micro-organism in the sandy soil below.

The museum is not for the faint-hearted. Anyone expecting cartoon mummies, carefully swaddled, will be disappointed – these are gruesome, naked, desiccated dead bodies, often painfully exhibiting the means by which they died. There are two French soldiers, one of whom was hanged, the other tortured; a Chinese couple who came to Italy for their honeymoon in 1750, caught cholera and never went back; and a bell ringer knocked off the tower by his own bell, his tongue still between his teeth. Children killed by the plague, mothers, and a murdered lawyer fill the crypt of the church, along with several hundred human skulls.

To get there, head across the piazza in the part of town to the east of the river – the ticket office is just down the road from the church.

Norcia → *For listings, see pages 76-86.*

High in the hills in the southeast of Umbria, and right at the edge of the Monti Sibillini National Park, Norcia is a different sort of town from its counterparts down on the plain. Famous for its truffles, its butchers and St Benedict, who was born here in AD 480, it has a strong identity of its own and feels like a solid mountain town, braced against earthquakes and the cold wind.

Despite being surrounded by wooded hills and valleys, the town centre is, unusually, flat. It was probably settled by the Sabines in the fifth century BC; as Nursia, it was an ally of Rome in the second Punic War in 205 BC. The 14th-century walls surrounding the town remain more or less intact, despite several destructive earthquakes.

Benedict and Scholastica

St Benedict was born in Norcia in AD 480. The only source work about his life is the second book of Pope Gregory I, written 50 years after Benedict's death. It tells how he went to study in Rome but was so appalled by the state of life there, at the tail end of the Roman Empire, that he became a hermit, and then an abbot to a group of monks. After a while, they became fed up with his reforms and tried to poison him, at which point he left them and set up his own small monasteries, including one at Montecassino, where he wrote his 'Rule': a set of guidelines that has been adopted and used by monks and nuns ever since. Much less is known about his twin sister Scholastica, and some have suggested that she is merely a personification of the Benedictine love of study.

The surrounding countryside is some of Umbria's wildest, with the hills of the Monti Sibillini National Park coming right down to the eastern edge of the town. To the north, the isolated Valcastoriana runs up the edge of the park, with some good walking possibilities and easy access to some of the region's most spectacular landscapes.

Arriving in Norcia

Getting there There are seven buses a day to Norcia from Spoleto, the nearest station. A car is useful, especially for getting out into the hills, though the winding roads can be slippery and dangerous.

Getting around There is free parking outside Porta Romana, at the northeast edge of town. Fairly frequent buses run to and from Spoleto (where you can transfer to the train) from outside Porta Ascolana.

Tourist information Tourist information office ① *piazza San Benedetto, T0743-817090, Tue-Fri 0930-1230, Sat-Sun 0930-1230, 1530-1830 (may be closed in winter).*

Piazza San Benedetto

Norcia's central piazza is an impressive if not entirely cohesive ensemble of buildings, consisting of a castle-turned-museum, a beautiful church and the 14th-century town hall. The information office for the Monti Sibillini National Park is also here. In the centre stands an 1880 statue of the town's most famous son, St Benedict (see box, above), founder of the Benedictine order and patron saint of Europe. The **Palazzo Comunale** has a portico that was added in 1492 and an attached chapel reached up steps from the piazza.

Basilica di San Benedetto

① *Piazza San Benedetto, T0743-817090, daily 0900-1800, free.*
On the corner of the piazza, to the right of the Palazzo Comunale, the church that marks the birthplace of the first Western monk and the first nun – Benedict and his twin sister Scholastica – is a strangely downbeat place. The Gothic façade has an attractive rose window as well as statues of the twins, but the interior has largely been rebuilt and has a disappointingly forgotten air. Downstairs it is more interesting, with a semi-excavated Roman house and some *opus reticulatum* Roman walls built into the crypt, which also has an ancient fresco.

Castellina and Museo Civico

① *Piazza San Benedetto, T0743-817030, www.artenorcia.net, Wed-Mon 1000-1300, 1600-1930, €4.*

Built by the papacy in 1554 to quell Norcian unruliness, the Castellina broods over the centre of the town and now holds its museum. There are medieval sculptures in stone and painted wood, and a terracotta *Madonna* by Luca della Robbia. Paintings include a rather feminine 15th-century *Risen Christ* and a Renaissance *Madonna and Child Enthroned* by Francesco Sparapane from 1530.

Duomo

Norcia's 16th-century cathedral, just off the **Piazza San Benedetto**, is a fairly dull church worth going into for the fresco of St Benedict and St Scholastica, alongside the Madonna and a redheaded Jesus, in the Cappella della Misericordia.

Several of the town's other churches are worth a peek inside if they're open: **San Giovanni** has a Renaissance altar, and the **Oratorio di Sant'Agostinuccio** has a nice wooden ceiling. The **Tempietto** is a small, square 14th-century shrine with arches opening on to the street, decorated with bas-relief.

Valcastoriana → *For listings, see pages 76-86.*

North of Norcia, this valley running along the edge of the national park is an isolated slice of rural central Italy, punctuated by abbeys and small villages perched precariously on the hillsides. Shepherds steer their flocks of sheep around, tractors plough the fields, and not very much else happens.

The road to **Preci**, running through the valley, forms the western border of the park, with villages such as **Campi Vecchio** perched above it on the west-facing slopes of the mountains. Despite the altitude, the landscape here is rolling rather than craggy, pastoral rather than dramatic, but it is a beautiful, peaceful place – it's not hard to see why monks and hermits chose to live here.

The **Abbazia di Sant'Eutizio** ① *T0743-99659*, is a good spot to aim for, about 20 minutes' drive out of Norcia. An important Benedictine abbey, it was built on an older Roman site in the fifth century. There's a **restaurant** ① *T074-393 9319, Tue-Sun*, a **museum** ① *Mon and Wed-Sat 1000-1300, 1500-1900, Sun 1000-1800, Sun only in winter, €2*, containing the abbey's treasures and remnants of the days when it was a noted centre for medicine, plus doves and peacocks, caves, a garden with views, and a church dating back to 1190.

En route, stop at the **Chiesa di San Salvatore**, below Campi Vecchio, for a look at its Gothic façade and 15th-century frescoes inside. A tree-lined road leads up the hill from here, with great views.

Monti Silbillini → *For listings, see pages 76-86.*

The region's wildest and most beautiful landscapes are in the **Monti Sibillini National Park** (www.sibillini.net), spilling across the border between Umbria and Marche. One of the highest parts of the Apennines, it is home to boar, wolves and a bear, and the backdrop to many legends of witchcraft and sorcery. Huge upland plains stretch out beneath its high snowy peaks, carpeted in spring and early summer with wild flowers and farmed at other times for lentils. At the heart of this wilderness, Castelluccio is a remote hill town, often cut off in winter and a great centre for walking and hang-gliding.

The Sibillini Sybil

The Sibyls were prophetesses in both Greek and Roman antiquity. Living in caves, they foresaw wars and the coming of Christianity and were consulted by emperors. Pictured on Michelangelo's Sistine Chapel ceiling, they may be the ancient forerunners of the relatively modern concept of the witch. Various myths put their number at 10 or 12. The so-called Apennine Sibyl, after whom the Sibillini Mountains are named, may not have been recognized as one of them during Roman times, though it's also possible that she was the Sibyl of Cumae, the most important Roman sibyl.

Medieval tradition says that she was a prophetess condemned to live in a mountain cave until Judgment Day because she threw a wobbly at the news that Mary had been chosen rather than her to be the mother of Jesus. It was believed that a coterie of beautiful young women lived with the enchantress in the mountain and would sometimes come out at night to dance with local young men, returning to their cave before dawn. So strong were some of these myths that the papacy found it necessary to forbid people to approach the cave, and later blocked off its entrance.

The River Nera cuts a narrow valley – the Valnerina – into the hills, a beautifully wooded place winding down from the Sibillini Mountains, with occasional ancient churches along its banks. ▶▶ *For activities in the national park, see What to do, page 85.*

Arriving in Monti Sibillini

Getting there Castelluccio is almost impossible to reach without a car. There are once-in-a-blue-moon buses from Norcia, but you might never get to leave. If you have no transport, a better bet might be hitching.

Tourist information Before visiting the Sibillini, contact one of the **Case del Parco** ⓘ *in Norcia, for example: piazza San Benedetto, T0743-817090,* to pick up official guides and maps. Or visit Castelluccio's **information centre** ⓘ *piazza di Castelluccio, T333-384 2646, but it's only open Jun to mid-Jul Sat-Sun 0930-1230, 1530-1830, mid-Jul to Aug daily 0930-1230, 1530-1830.*

Castelluccio and the Piano Grande

Despite all the postcards and calendar shots, it's hard to be prepared for the Piano Grande. A gargantuan grassy basin between high mountains, it sprouts a profusion of wild flowers in late spring and early summer. Later, in autumn, as the beech woods turn a thousand shades of orange and rust brown, it is often filled with a sea of morning fog, out of which the hill village of **Castelluccio**, one of Italy's highest inhabited places, pokes into the bright sunshine. In winter it is often bitterly cold, and snow blankets the surrounding hills, some of which have gentle ski runs. Used mostly for grazing sheep and cows, and for growing lentils, it is a serene place, with occasional walkers and hang-gliders punctuating the vast open spaces.

Castelluccio is a tough, frost-bitten sort of place, with little or none of the cuteness found at lower levels. The views are extraordinary, and though there are no obvious sights, the village's situation alone is enough to make it a must-see. In 2008 every street was dug up to lay new cables and pipes, bringing fibre optics to houses that until recently

Ulysses and his taste for honey

A rare Marsican brown bear, Ulysses was discovered in the Monti Sibillini National Park in 2007, having arrived from Abruzzo to the south.

Adult Marsican brown bears weigh as much as 130 kg and are nearly 2 m tall when standing on their hind legs. Traces of Ulysses' presence were found on apple trees that he had climbed, and he damaged a number of beehives in his search for honey. Photo traps have recorded him a number of times, and about 14 km of tracks have been followed. It is believed that his Sibillini territory covers an area of over 330 sq km, though he has also ventured outside the park. He probably hibernates in a remote mountain cave.

If he's still there, his existence in the national park is likely to remain a lonely one. The Marsican brown bear is one of the most critically endangered of European mammal species and – apart from Ulysses – is believed to exist only in the Abruzzo National Park, where the total population numbers only about 40.

It's thought that many bears have been deliberately poisoned in Abruzzo.

had no electricity – it remains to be seen whether such progress will drag Castelluccio into the 21st century.

All around the Piano Grande there is fantastic walking territory. The Kompass 1:50,000 Sibillini map is one of the easiest to get hold of; the tourist information office in Norcia sells a rather flimsy alternative, or you may be able to find a 1:25,000 CAI map. There are paths, but it's also possible to walk just about anywhere across the unfenced mountains.

For those looking for a longer trek, there are plenty of routes following the Appenine ridge north from Castelluccio, and there's a circuit of the national park known as the **Grande Anello** ('big ring') – a nine-day, 120-km route. Information centres have a good booklet (in English) on the route and there are *rifugi* (refuges) on the way round. For mountain bikers, there's a longer, 160-km route, taking four or five days and also called the Grande Anello.

Lago di Pilato

Just below the ring of the Sibillini's highest peaks, the Lake of Pontius Pilate is said to contain his body. Some stories say that he drowned himself here, others that his body was driven by oxen into the lake. The rare freshwater crayfish that live here, and occasionally turn the water red, add to the mythology surrounding the place. At a height of 1940 m, it is hidden between Monte Vettore and Cima del Redentore, but can be reached by walking from the end of the road leading northeast out of Castelluccio (12 km there and back). From the road, head east to the pass of Forca Viola before turning south up the Valle del Lago di Pilato.

Valle Umbra and southeast Umbria listings

For hotel and restaurant price codes and other relevant information, see pages 11-15.

🛏 Where to stay

Spello *p58*

€€€ Albergo del Teatro, via Giulia 24, T0742-301140, www.hoteldelteatro.it. The breakfast terrace with great views is the highlight of this comfortable, mid-range hotel, with 11 rooms, in the centre of Spello. There are shiny wooden floors, tiled bathrooms (some with jacuzzis), peach-coloured walls and big beds.

€€€ Il Sommelier, via Porta Fontevecchia, T0742-21410, www.residenzailsommelier. com. This B&B has 4 suites, each loosely themed around a wine. Wooden rafters, bare stone walls, tiled floors and fireplaces add to the appeal; breakfast is served in the ex-wine cellar.

€€€ La Bastiglia, via Salnitraria 15, T0742-651277, www.labastiglia.com. Closed 9 Jan-9 Feb. Spello's most stylish accommodation, La Bastiglia, at the top of the town, has a beautifully landscaped swimming pool with great views over the Chiona Valley. There are 3 grades of room, the best ('not unlike royal residences') having private terraces; the junior suites also have hot tubs. Rooms in the new wing have less character but all have shiny wooden floors and comfortable, modern furnishings. Half board, at €35 extra per person, with dinner in the hotel's smart restaurant (see page 79), is a good deal.

€€€ Palazzo Bocci, via Cavour 17, T0742-301021, www.palazzobocci.com. A 14th-century building decorated in 19th-century style: the best of the 23 rooms have frescoes and open fires, though most are much plainer. From Jun to Sep the buffet breakfast is served in the garden. Satellite TV and a/c.

Self-catering

Buonanotte Barbanera, via Fonte del Mastro II 9, T0335-354597, www.buonanotte barbanera.it. Exceedingly stylish, this townhouse-for-rent is halfway between an Umbrian hideaway and a Moroccan riad. There's a beautiful walled garden and the 3 elegant double bedrooms have colourful fabrics and carefully chosen art. Wood, white walls, tiles and brick vaulting all contribute and there's a kitchen in a more rural style, with painted dressers. It's available for rent in its entirety for a minimum stay of a week (€500 per day in high season). Up the hill, smaller **La Casetta** repeats the refined style. **In Urbe**, via Giulia 97, T0742-301145, www.inurbe.it. Simple but attractive self-catering apartments in the centre of Spello, with wooden floors, some exposed brick, and good views across the countryside. Kitchens have fridges and gas cookers. Certainly not Spello's most luxurious accommodation but very good value, and they'll pick you up from the station too.

Bevagna *p61*

€€€€ Orto degli Angeli, via Dante Alighieri 1, T0742-360130, www.ortoangeli. it. A grand townhouse from the 18th century and a Renaissance palace make up this stunning hotel in the heart of the old Roman town. There is a pretty hanging garden built over the Roman theatre, which incorporates some of the original walls. The rooms in the 18th-century building are formal and smart, with frescoed ceilings, while the older building has a more relaxed, rustic feel. Everywhere there are generous public spaces, and thoughtful design infuses the hotel.

€€€ Genius Loci, via Monti Martani 23, T0742-362111, www.geniuslociumbria.com. Outside Bevagna, en route to Montefalco, **Genius Loci** is a handsome country house with a pool. Cookery courses and wine tastings are on offer.

€€ Il Chiostro di Bevagna, corso Matteotti 107, T0742-361987, www.ilchiostrodibevagna.com. Set around a cloister just off the piazza, large wooden furniture and corny Alpine scenes decorate spacious, comfortable rooms. The whole place has a slightly down-at-heel feeling, but it's good value, and in summer the buffet breakfast is served in the cloister itself.

Montefalco *p62*

€€€ Villa Pambuffetti, viale della Vittoria 20, T0742-379417, www.villapambuffetti.com. Just outside the city walls, in tree-filled grounds, **Pambuffetti** has a pool and some great views of the surrounding countryside, especially from the sought-after tower bedroom, plus wood panelling, a/c and an outdoor summer restaurant under a gazebo. There are lots of books and a fire in the reception area, and cookery classes can be booked on site.

€€ Camiano Piccolo, via Camiano Piccolo 5, T0742-379492, www.camianopiccolo.com. About 1 km downhill out of town, this *agriturismo* has 9 comfortable rooms and 6 apartments in ex-farm buildings around a pool and shaded by trees. In the summer you can eat alfresco, whereas in winter there's a cosy wooden-beamed interior in country farmhouse style. The menu is traditional Umbrian with no real surprises, but service is friendly and the place has a nice relaxed air. Apartments are available to rent on a weekly basis, rooms by the night. Rooms in the house have more style than those in the outbuildings.

€€ Hotel degli Affreschi, corso Mameli 45, T0742-379243. A friendly, family-run place in the centre of town, with good views and some 17th-century frescoes. Recently refurbished, it's comfortable and very well placed. Guests also get free access to the pool at the modern hotel **Nuovo Mondo**, outside the town.

Trevi *p63*

€€€ Antica Dimora alla Rocca, piazza della Rocca, T0742-38541, www.hotel allarocca.it. In a handsome 17th-century building in the middle of Trevi, the 34 rooms of this elegant and friendly hotel are split between the *piano nobile* – the 1st floor, with frescoes and high ceilings – and the old servants' quarters on the less fussy 2nd floor, with wooden beams and a cosier feel. Breakfast is served right on the intimate piazza della Rocca.

Spoleto *p65, map p66*

During the festival, Spoleto's hotels fill up and prices rise; book well in advance.

€€€ Gattapone, via del Ponte 6, T0743-223447, www.hotelgattapone.it. Elegant, arty and with an undertone of decadence, **Gattapone** has 15 rooms near the *rocca*, and great views over the Ponte delle Torri and the valley below. The American bar has old festival posters and an early 20th-century feel, while downstairs in the lounge there are deep red walls, leather sofas and big windows. Rooms are slightly plainer but very comfortable. Free parking.

€€€ Palazzo Dragoni, via del Duomo 13, T0743-222220, www.palazzodragoni.it. In an ancient town house overlooking the Valle Umbra, **Palazzo Dragoni** has a grand sitting room with a piano, a breakfast room with views all the way to Assisi, and smart rooms with parquet floors, arches, and more vistas, for which it's sometimes not even necessary to get out of bed. Ask to see the secret tunnels under the house, which once led people to food and safety in times of siege.

€€€ Palazzo Leti, via degli Eremiti 10, T0743-224930, www.palazzoleti.com. At the top of town, **Palazzo Leti** is an elegant hotel with a formal garden overlooking the valley (and, unfortunately, the road) to the east. The 11 rooms are warm, cosy and stylish, with metal-framed beds, tiles, antiques, old beams and modern luxuries such as a/c and, in some cases, jacuzzis. All rooms face the valley.

€€ Hotel Charleston, piazza Collicola 10, T0743-220052, www.hotelcharleston.it. Stylish and good value, the **Charleston** is a 17th-century building with a bar and wine-tasting room, a sauna and a good communal space with a fireplace. Recently refurbished rooms are light and have muted colour schemes and some have views over the piazza.

€€ Il Panciolle, via del Duomo 3, T0743-45677, www.albergopanciolle.it. Generous and reliable rooms are comfortable and well kitted out, with TVs and minibars. Rooms overlooking the street aren't very bright – those facing the valley are better. A simple breakfast is included and there's a popular restaurant downstairs.

Around Spoleto p69

€€€ Le Terre di Poreta, località Poreta, T0743-521186, www.leterrediporeta.it. 11 km north of Spoleto. A 17th-century organic olive oil estate, **Le Terre** have turned various buildings into guest accommodation – whether you want an apartment or a 7-bedroomed villa they have it. And all come with access to swimming pools, tennis courts, and a gym with a sauna. There is also the chance to join in estate activities such as pruning the olives or going truffle hunting.

€€€ San Pietro in Valle, Ferentillo, 22 km southeast of Spoleto, T0744-780129, www.sanpietroinvalle.com. May-Oct. Sympathetically restored rooms are grouped around the cloister of a beautiful abbey in the Valnerina. The 19 rooms and 2 suites have old tiled floors, wooden furniture and beams. Some of the larger rooms also have their own seating areas. A beautiful grassy garden faces across the valley towards the ruined village of Umbriano. The nearby **Santa Croce Agriturismo**, www.santacroceagriturismo.it, with 7 apartments based around a 14th-century tower with a swimming pool, is under the same management.

Norcia p71

€€€ Il Casale degli Amici, vocabolo Cappuccini 157, T0743- 816811, www.ilcasaledegliamici.it. A lentil-growing farm with beautiful rustic rooms and apartments in a peaceful spot about 3 km east of Norcia. Rooms are very nicely kitted out with solid wood furniture and metal-framed beds, and the welcome is exceptionally warm, as is the underfloor heating. Half board is a good option, as the attached restaurant (see page 83) serves some of Norcia's best food; breakfast is special too, with lots of home-made produce. Larger rooms are worth paying the extra €10 for – well designed, they have fireplaces, seating areas and big wooden beds.

€€€ Palazzo Seneca, via Cesare Battisti 12, T0743-817434, www.palazzoseneca.com. Norcia's newest and most stylish accommodation, **Palazzo Seneca** is a 'residenza di charme' opened in 2008 after 10 years of rebuilding and redesigning. It's an elegant hotel in a 17th-century palace with a jazz bar (concerts are usually held every Sat night), a library, a refined restaurant and a stylish wellness centre in the cellar complete with sauna, marble massage parlour and a chromotherapy bath. Suites have black marble bathrooms, and there are nice touches such as antique phones.

€€ Casale nel Parco, vocabolo Fontevena 8, 1 km outside Norcia on the way to Fontevena, T0743-816481, www.casalenelparco.com. Catering for walkers, **Casale nel Parco** has a good swimming pool under the hills and some simply decorated and fairly rustic rooms and apartments, with plenty of space for a family, that open on to a central grassy area. There's a restaurant with a large fireplace, they offer traditional *prete* (bed-warmers) and can organize horse-riding trips.

€€ Grotta Azzurra, corso Sertorio 24, T0743-816513, www.bianconi.com. Should the **Palazzo Seneca** be full, or too expensive, this nearby hotel, owned by the same family, would be a reasonable fall-back, especially if you can get one of the better, bigger rooms with tented beds. Smaller, more modern rooms upstairs have balconies, but the style feels a little dated.

Monti Sibillini p73

Castelluccio's only 'proper' hotel is the basic **Albergo Sibilla** – the **Locanda de' Senari** is a much better option.

€€ La Locanda de' Senari, via della Bufera, T0743-821205, www.agriturismosenari.it. 25 Apr-Oct, and weekends in winter. On the edge of the village, with great views over the Piano Grande, **Locanda de' Senari** is a cosy *agriturismo* with 5 attractive rooms and a restaurant offering good, traditional meals using home-grown ingredients. The menu changes regularly, but always includes lentils and local meats. Some rooms have 4-poster beds and there are sloping, wooden-beamed ceilings and large showers. Downstairs there's a roaring open fire.

€€ La Vecchia Stalla, Astorara, T0736-41758, www.benale.net. In a village on the Marche side of Monte Vettore, this is an attractive thick-walled stone mountain B&B with a very warm welcome. Spectacularly perched 1000 m up, there are excellent walks from the front door. There are just 2 double rooms. The family owns an organic farm, which supplies some of the ingredients for the excellent home-cooked food.

🍴 Restaurants

Spello p58

€€€€ La Bastiglia, via Salnitraria 15, T0742-651277, www.labastiglia.com. Wed-Mon 1300-1415, 2000-2230, closed Thu lunch and 9 Jan-9 Feb. A swish but unexpectedly relaxed restaurant, with dark wooden ceilings and big contemporary art, which spreads out from its 3 rooms on to the terrace in summer. **La Bastiglia** offers set menus with extravagant titles such as 'a journey through the balanced senses'. If the name, the 8 courses or the suckling pig seem a little over the top, you could go for the vegetarian menu, with more down-to-earth dishes such as chickpea flan with red turnip sauce.

€€€ Drinking Wine, via Garibaldi 20, T0742-301625, www.drinkingwine.it. Thu-Tue 1100-2400. Sunk down from the main street, you can do as the name says at this modern wine bar, though they also serve coffee, pear and chocolate tart and some good light meals such as potato, rosemary and chicken salad. In summer there are more tables across the street under umbrellas.

€€€ Enoteca Properzio, piazza Matteotti 8/10, T0742-301521, www.enoteche.it. Daily 1000-2200. One of Umbria's finest *enoteche*, **Properzio** stocks 2200 different wines, and provides good food to go along with them. In the 12th- and 13th-century Palazzo dei Canonici in the centre of Spello, one of the wine-tasting rooms was once used as a studio by Pinturicchio. There are tables outside on the street, inside under brick-vaulted ceilings, and in a walled garden at the back. Try the exceptionally good bruschette selection, or the carefully sourced Mediterranean salad with 35-year-old balsamic vinegar. Wine tastings are available (in good English); book in advance by phone or email and allow €40-60 per person for a couple of hours, food included.

€€€ Il Molino, piazza Matteotti 6/7, T0742-651305. Wed-Mon 1215-1430, 1930-2240. An atmospheric spot, in a 14th-century oil mill, **Il Molino** has an open fire, brick-vaulted ceiling, white tablecloths and wooden chairs, and serves traditional Umbrian dishes such as grilled meats, pasta, and soups with wild asparagus and a certain amount of style.

€€€ La Cantina di Spello, via Cavour 2, T0742-651775, www.oasiumbria.it. Tue-Sun lunch and dinner. Attached to a shop selling fine foods from the region, **La Cantina** uses the same local ingredients to good effect in its smart restaurant. The menu is seasonal but may include dishes such as swordfish 'bites' with capers and olives or Lake Trasimeno bean salad.

€€ Osteria de Dadà, via Cavour 47, T0742-301327. Mon-Sat 1230-1530, 1900-2230, Sun 1230-1530. A friendly little place with simple wooden tables, where they're keen on doing things the right – and Umbrian – way. The locally sourced menu changes daily, and depends on what's in season. Specialities include *cinghiale sagrantino* (wild boar cooked in red wine), and pasta is always home-made, either tagliatelle or *strangozzi*. There's a set 3-course menu for €18, but the owner is happy for you to order as little or as much as you like.

Cafés and bars
Bar Giardino Bonci, via Garibaldi 10, T0742-651397. Thu-Tue summer 0700-2400, winter 0700-2230. As a restaurant it may not be especially exciting, but its garden, with superlative views, makes this a great spot for a drink or an ice cream.

Bevagna *p61*
€€€ La Bodega di Assù, corso Matteotti 102, T0742-360978. Thu-Tue 1130-2100, closed 10 Jan-end Feb. Just off the main square, **Assù**'s bodega is a friendly, chirpy, effortlessly cool place, tiny but packed with interesting things to look at, with arty photos, piles of books, colouring pencils on every table, handwritten menus and wine bottles lining the walls. There are also 2 or 3 tables outside on the street. The food is great too – try a fresh, succulent, wild leaf salad, or a hearty fennel and celery soup. You can also buy produce to take home: wine, olive oil, and even the ceramic jugs that water is served from.
€€€ Ottavius, via Gonfalone 4, T0742-360555, www.ottavius.it. Tue-Sun 1230-1430, 1930-2230. Sunk down below the level of the piazza, Ottavius is famous for its *gnocchi al sagrantino*, but you might also go for the mixed grill with broad bean purée. It has bare walls and a friendly atmosphere.
€€€ Redibis, via dell'Anfiteatro, T0742-360130, www.redibis.it. Thu-Mon 1230-1430, 1930-2200, Wed 1930-2200. Built into the

structure of the ancient Roman theatre, **Redibis** is a large, grand place, with elegant hanging lights and plenty of style. From the entrance you circle around what would once have been the stage until you come to a cavernous dining room. Try the fresh, home-made pasta with bacon and tomato, and save some room for pears marinated in Montefalco wine. There is a tasting menu for €45.

Cafés and bars
Caffè Farfalle, piazza Garibaldi. Good home-made ice cream in summer.

Montefalco *p62*
€€€ Il Coccorone, largo Tempestivi, T0742-379535, www.coccorone.com. Thu-Tue 1230-1430, 1930-2200. A smart place with a handful of outdoor tables with geraniums, and white tableclothed tables inside under brick arches and wooden beams. The open fire is lit even in summer to cook the meat that dominates the menu. There's a cheaper 'tourist menu' as well as the extensive *menu degustazione*. Truffles, guinea fowl and snails all feature and, though it can feel a little dated, standards are high.
€€€ L'Alchimista, piazza del Comune 14, T0742-378558, www.montefalcowines.com. Wed-Mon 1230-1500, 1900-2145, Tue 1230-1500. With wooden tables right on the central piazza, **l'Alchimista** is a cool, chic, family-run wine bar with exceptionally good food. There's a good range of salads, such as radicchio with grilled pecorino, pear and walnuts, and a fine selection of polenta made from various grains. Unusually good vegetarian options include *lasagne alchimista* – stuffed crêpe with radicchio, porcini mushrooms and cheese. Jazzy Italian music comes from an iPod-dock, and a vine climbs up the cooling pergola. It's popular and hardly a secret, so arrive early or reserve a table.
€€€ Spiritodivino, piazza Mustafà 2, T0742-379048, www.spiritodivino.net. Tue-Sun 0900-0100, daily in Aug. A chic

sort of wine bar, **Spiritodivino** cultivates a tastefully sinful atmosphere, with contemporary styling such as chilli plants on the outdoor tables and a large black and white photo of naked women drinking wine on one of the inside walls. Dishes such as honeyed cod on sliced tomato and Chianina beef are well matched with the wide selection of Umbrian wines.

€€ Il Verziere, via Goffredo Mameli 22, T0742-379166, www.ringhieraumbra.com. Tue-Sun lunch and dinner. Minimalist interior design has yet to reach **Il Verziere**, where every inch of wall and ceiling is covered in pictures, signs and musical instruments. Service and cuisine is straightforward rather than inventive, but there are wood-fired pizzas, as well as pastas, risottos and plenty of local wine.

Trevi *p63*

€€€ Gustavo, via Salita San Francesco 13, T0742-78545, www.gustavogustavino.it. Tue-Sun 1830-0130. A wine bar with candles in wine bottles on wooden tables, live music and poetry, and home-made dishes, such as gnocchi with radicchio, and goat's cheese with strawberry compote, chalked up on a board. There's also a tasting menu for €25.

€€€ La Prepositura, vicolo Oscuro 2a, T0742-381392, www.hotelallarocca.it. Daily 1200-1400, 1945-2215. **La Prepositura** offers an interesting menu in vaulted rooms just off the piazza. Dishes may include smoked turkey carpaccio and veal with lemon and there's a good value €14, 3-course lunch menu.

€€€ La Vecchia Posta, piazza Mazzini 14, T0742-381690, www.lavecchiaposta.net. Fri-Wed 1230-1500, 1930-2200. On the main piazza, **La Vecchia Posta** serves carefully presented traditional Umbrian food such as pappardelle with wild boar or capelletti with truffles, and good, home-made desserts. It's a cosy, friendly, yellow-walled place, with a few tables outside on the piazza in summer. Upstairs there are rooms for rent.

€€ Gustavino, piazza Mazzini 7, no phone. Tue-Sun 1030-2300. A wine bar with pretty slatted folding wooden tables under umbrellas outside. Chic styling includes wine-based axioms written on the tables, pink-on-black handwritten menus and orange water glasses. Excellent salads are served on large wooden platters with wooden cutlery and there's superb coffee too.

Cafés and bars

Caffè Roma, piazza Mazzini. In the corner of the piazza, **Caffè Roma** is where the locals come to chat and while away the day. It may not be the world's most atmospheric café, but its position, just under the tower, means it does a steady trade.

Spoleto *p65, map p66*

€€€ Cantina de' Corvi, piazzetta Santi Giovanni e Paolo, T0743-44475, www.cantinadecorvi.it. Tue-Sun 1230-1500, 1930-2230. Tables outside on a wooden platform under cover, and a smaller, vaulted space inside. It's popular with Italians, and the four-course 'menu del territorio', including lamb, the traditional local *strangozzi* pasta and wine, is a good deal.

€€€ Emporio, via Porta Fuga 22, T0743-47623. Lunchtime and Fri-Sun evenings. A lively place, with a mix of old-fashioned rural style and playful modern colour. There are a couple of tables outside, as well as some metal picnic tables inside among the wine bottles and vegetables. The menu of the day gets posted on the door.

€€€ Il Panciolle, vicolo degli Eroli 1, T0743-221241, www.ilpanciolle.it. Daily 1230-1430, 1930-2230 (closed Wed in winter). Underneath the hotel of the same name, **Panciolle** has an open grill on which meat is cooked, and a large garden with palm trees and views. Popular with locals, it's decorated with greens and yellows and has open stonework and arches. There's a wide selection of wines, and they are carefully matched to the food, which changes often – expect traditional Umbrian dishes with a degree of flair, excellent local cheeses and a good choice of breads.

€€€ Il Tempio del Gusto, via Arco di Druso 11, T0743-47121, www.iltempiodelgusto.com. Fri-Wed 1030-1500, 1800-2400. 'The Temple of Taste' has tables outside in summer on the piazza as well as intimate rooms inside. There are daily specials and good set options, including a vegetarian menu. The bread is warm, the waiting staff glamorous. Presentation is clearly important here, and antipasti come with artistically arranged elements on square black plates. Try the smoked trout and salmon or the delicious wholewheat pasta with pigeon in a Sagrantino sauce. There are good home-made desserts too.

€€€ Osteria del Matto, vicolo del Mercato 3, T0743-225506. Wed-Sat 1100-1500, 1700-0200, Sun 1100-1500, 1700-1200. A little like participatory theatre, at the 'Osteria of the Madman' the eccentric and vivacious host will draw you in to an extraordinary piece of drama in which he is the protagonist. There's no menu – the only question is whether you want white or red wine. You'll get a series of small courses of delicious Umbrian dishes, from green salad to pork with cheese sauce to fried courgette flowers. After a couple of courses you'll feel like an old friend and after a couple more you'll feel full. But there may be another half dozen to come, so pace yourself. All this comes in at a very reasonable fixed price, plus wine.

€€€ Osteria del Trivio, via del Trivio 16, T0743-44349. Wed-Mon 1230-1430, 1930-2200. Decorated in Umbrian country-kitchen style, with red-and-white checked tablecloths, tiled floor, dresser and old weighing scales. Specials change daily and you'll probably be given a choice at your table rather than presented with a menu. The *strangozzi* pasta with broad beans, bacon and pecorino is excellent.

€€€ Tric Trac, piazza Duomo 10, T0743-44592. Daily 1200-1600, 1830 till late. On the edge of the piazza facing the *duomo*, Tric Trac is a smart but not too formal

enoteca and a good spot to sit with a glass of wine and appreciate the *duomo*. There are 2 menus – a lighter, faster *enoteca* menu and a restaurant menu; you can order from either or both. The salad Caravaggio, with pear, white cabbage, chicory and fennel in a limoncello dressing, is especially good, and a whole section of the menu is devoted to black truffles.

€€ L'Angolo Antico, via Monterone 109, T0743-49066. Tue-Sun lunch and dinner. A large Italian place with old festival posters and banknotes decorating the walls. The menu is extensive and includes decent if rather thin pizzas as well as main courses such as snails, wild boar casserole, and the ubiquitous pasta with spicy tomato *spolentina* sauce. The mixed bruschette are excellent and local families munch along happily to piped Italian pop.

Cafés and bars

Gelateria Primavera, piazza del Mercato 7, T0743-48580. A wide selection of home-made ice cream right on one of Spoleto's main piazzas. It fills up with locals in the evenings.

Il Mio Vinaio, via Arco di Druso 8, T0743-49893. Daily 0900-2100. Just off piazza Mercato, this is a good spot for a lunchtime wooden platter of meats and cheeses with a glass or 2 of local wine.

Osteria dell'Enoteca, via Saffi 7, T0743-220484, www.osteriadellenoteca.com. Wed-Mon 1100-1500, 1900-2300. Good traditional food as well as plenty of wine choices at this dark, atmospheric little spot.

Around Spoleto *p69*

€€€€ Al Cantico, Abbazia di San Pietro in Valle, Ferentillo, 22 km southeast of Spoleto, T0744-780005, www.ilcantico.it. Lunch from 1200, dinner from 1800, closed Mon lunch and Dec-Mar. Under separate ownership from the neighbouring hotel, **Cantico** keeps its customers happy with high-quality food. There are 4 different set menus from €50-60.

€€€ Osteria Baciafemmine, vicolo Baciafemmine, Scheggino, 13 km southeast of Spoleto on SS209, T0743-618311, www.osteriabaciafemmine.it. Thu-Tue evenings, Sun lunch. An *osteria* in the pretty riverside village of Scheggino. The name comes from the fact that the alley is so narrow that passers-by cannot help but kiss. It's a cosy place, using seasonal ingredients, and meat is roasted on the open fire.

Norcia *p71*
€€€ Granaro del Monte, via Alfieri 10, T0743-817551. Daily lunch and dinner. Norcia's most popular restaurant, underneath the **Grotta Azzurra** hotel, is a huge place, with cosy rooms inside, near the roaring fire, or tables outside. Meat cooked on the open fire is the speciality but there are plenty of truffle and lentil dishes too.
€€€ Il Casale degli Amici, vocabolo Cappuccini 157, T328-861 2385, www.ilcasa ledegliamici.it. 1245-1500, 1945-2130; may be closed during the week in winter – ring ahead to check. Up the hill out of Norcia, **Casale degli Amici** is an *agriturismo* (see page 78) with a fantastic restaurant. The lentils are home grown, the salami is of the highest quality, the pasta is melt-in-your-mouth fresh and the meat is expertly cooked. In a large, barrel-vaulted room with bare stonework and lights suspended from wires, it's also an atmospheric place, and one that is popular with locals. Well worth the trip.
€€€ Taverna de' Massari, via Roma 13, T0743-816218, www.tavernademassari.com. Wed-Mon lunch and dinner. This little place just off piazza Santi Forti has checked tablecloths and a 'typical' menu22, or you could splash out on a truffle menu34 for €46. A la carte dishes such as tortellini with cream and truffles, or Castelluccio lentils with grilled sausage, are hearty and typically Norcian.
€€ Trattoria del Francese, via Riguardati 16, T0743-816290. Sat-Thu (daily Jul-Sep) 1200-1430 (1500 in summer), 1930-2130. A small place with an open fire on which the meat is cooked, **Trattoria del Francese**

makes few concessions to stylishness – the wood cladding is ugly, there are polystyrene tiles on the ceiling, and shields, plates and certificates decorate the walls. The food, however, is excellent, and it fills up with loyal Italians. There's a separate truffle menu and the *contorni* are unusually good.

Monti Sibillini *p73*
In Castelluccio, **La Locanda de' Senari** (see page 79) also has a good restaurant.
€€ Panini allo Scarafischio, Castelluccio. What appears to be little more than a burger van in Castelluccio's piazza-cum-car-park is actually one of the best places around to buy fine sausages, cured meats and cheese, any of which can be made into great panini, hot or cold. Expect conversation about world economic problems and a plastic beaker of wine to go with your ham sandwich.
€€ Taverna Castelluccio, via Dietro la Torre 8, T0743-821158, www.taverna castelluccio.it. Homely and simple, with blue and white tablecloths, and pictures on the walls inside and a couple of tables outside on the street, the taverna offers a traditional local menu using almost all local, natural ingredients such as lentils, beans, beef and pecorino cheese.

☺ Festivals

Spoleto *p65, map p66*
Jun/Jul Festival dei Due Mondi, Spoleto, www.festivaldispoleto.com. 3-week music and opera festival including theatre, dance and visual arts performances. One of Italy's most important cultural events.

◯ Shopping

Spello *p58*
Art
Arte & Arte Applicata, via Cavour 13, T0742-652022, www.cucciarelli.eu. Easter-Oct daily 1000-1300, 1500-1800 (but if you phone to request a viewing in winter they'll be happy to open up for you). Whereas

many 'galleries' in the region try to sell tourist tat with an artistic veneer, this little place is full of imaginative and inventive pieces in wood made by local sculptor Angelo Cucciarelli. Some of his large sculptures are displayed here (ask to see the catalogue) among the charming chess sets, coat hooks and lamps, all beautifully crafted and with a playful sense of fun.

Food

Hispellum, corso Cavour 35, T0742-651766, www.enotecahispellum.com, has a great selection of local wine, cheese and meat, but **La Tavola dell'Umbro**, right on piazza della Repubblica, T0742-651340, Mon-Sat 0700-1330, 1530-1930, Sun 0900-1300, 1530-1900, is better for picnic provisions, with fruit, bread and a wide range of drinks as well as cheese and other regional produce.

Bevagna *p61*
Food and drink
La Casereccia, corso Matteotti 56, T0742-361969. Delicious home-made pasta is made at the back of this little shop on the main street.
L'Orto di Porta, piazza Garibaldi, T0742-360584. Good local fruit and veg.

Trevi *p63*
Kappa Market, via Lucarini 35, T0742-781145. Mon-Sat 0900-1300, 1630-2000. A little supermarket with bread, a deli counter, excellent fruit and veg and lots of good picnic fare, as well as locally produced olive oil in industrial-size cans.

Spoleto *p65, map p66*
Il Libro, corso Mazzini 63, T0743-46678. Mon-Sat 0930-1300, 1630-2000, Sun 1130-1300, 1800-2000. An excellent selection of books on Spoleto and Umbria – coffee-table photography books as well as guide books. Also some maps and English-language novels.
Mobilia, via Sahara Vecchia 30, T0743-45720. Daily 0900-1300, 1530-1930.

A good mix of old-fashioned metal toys, globes, mobiles, antique magnifying glasses and furniture.
Spoleto Galleria, via Arco di Druso 7, T0743-225873, www.spoletogalleria.it. Closed Thu morning. The sort of shop that Spoleto does very well: high-quality crafts, sculpture and furniture with a touch of imaginative eccentricity.

Norcia *p71*
Antica Norcineria, piazza del Comune 11. Daily 0700-1330, 1600-2000. A decent range of bread, cheese and fruit right in the middle of town. And there's an *enoteca* next door should you want a bottle of Sagrantino.

◑ What to do

Trevi *p63*
Walking
Trevi tourist information offers a free town map with walking routes in the area on the back. The **Cammino di San Francesco** goes through the town, and you could combine a walk along this with the **Sentiero degli Ulivi** to make a satisfying circuit of 2 or 3 hrs, with some good views.

Spoleto *p65, map p66*
Cycling
A 60-km route along the banks of streams and rivers, the **Spoleto–Assisi cycle path** starts at its highest point, in the village of Arezzo (not to be confused with the Tuscan town) near Spoleto. There is a dam on the River Marroggia here. Tourist information in Spoleto can provide you with a booklet detailing the route. Another cycle path runs along the valley floor on the far side of the main roads below Trevi.

The Lower Valnerina *p69*
Adventure
Parco Avventura Nahar, vocabolo Rosciano 25, Arrone, 8 km from the Cascate delle Marmore on road to Polino, T320-275 6657, www.lacollinafiocchi.com. Jul-Aug

daily 1000-1900, Mar-Jun and Sep-Nov Sat-Sun 1000 to 1 hr before sunset, €15, junior trail €10. Helmeted and attached to a wire, you clamber high up through the trees of the Valnerina on this adventure trail.

Rafting
Centro Canoa e Rafting Le Marmore, via Carlo Neri, T330-753420, www.rafting marmore.com. You can try whitewater rafting from just below the Marmore Falls, or a more gentle punt downstream from Ferentillo. Both trips last around an hour; neither requires any rafting experience, though you should be a good swimmer. All clothing and equipment is provided.

Monti Sibillini *p73*
The Monti Sibillini National Park is a great setting for year-round activities, from paragliding and hang-gliding, to cross-country skiing, walking or kite flying.

Cycling
Sibillini Cycling, in Sarnano, on the Marche side of the park, T334-743 8418, or T+44(0)208-133 5441 in the UK, www.sibillinicycling.com. Apr-Oct. Rents mountain bikes from €15 a day and offers free car cycle carriers and helmets. Also offers guided 'bike days' and short touring holidays.

Hang-gliding and paragliding
Prodelta, T339-563 5456, www.prodelta.it. Hang-gliders and paragliders flock from all over Europe to Castelluccio and the Piano Grande, where the vast expanses of grassy slopes and a large, smooth landing site make it a perfect spot for flying, especially for beginners.

Throwing yourself off the top of a mountain and gliding down on the thermals must be one of the best ways to see the Sibillini. No experience is necessary, and a tandem flight with an experienced, licenced glider gives you most of the exhilaration, without some of the fear.

Ring in advance to reserve a flight – 1 day's notice may be enough during the week, but you usually need to book at least 3 or 4 days ahead for weekend flights. It may sometimes be necessary to cancel flights because of bad weather.

Horse riding
Centro Ippico Oxer, Paganelli, about 7 km from Norcia, T339-533 4468, www.escursioniacavallo.it. The **Oxer** riding centre, offers excursions on horseback in the Sibillini, ranging from a gentle afternoon's walk to longer treks on ancient mountain tracks, camping or staying in refuges or on farms.

Rafting
Gaia, località Biselli di Norcia, T338-767 8308, www.asgaia.it. On the edge of the Sibillini, near Norcia, there are opportunities for rafting downstream on the Corno River, both slowly and quickly. If a meandering journey is more your thing, the Biselli Gorge is a good route, with opportunities to swim.

There are also rapids that can be tackled by those after a little more adrenaline, and places where the brave can dive into streams from a 'natural diving board'. **Rafting Umbria**, T348-351 1798, www.raftingumbria.com.

Skiing
There are ski lifts on **Colle le Cese**, to the south of Castelluccio, as well as at **Monte Prata**, to the north, and you can do cross-country skiing across the plains. It's a stunningly beautiful place to ski, though the slopes are relatively short and not especially steep. The snow can be unreliable, however, even in the middle of winter, and there is little infrastructure except at weekends.

Walking
For a serious trek, the **Grande Anello dei Sibillini** (Great Sibillini Ring) is a 120-km, 9-day route. The park website, www.sibillini.net, also has details (in Italian) of many 1-day walks you can do, or you can grab a decent

map (see page 74) and strike out on your own. Especially up high in the mountains it's possible to walk just about anywhere, but make sure you are properly equipped – it's quite possible for the weather to close in.

Monte Guiadone, near Castelluccio
From the belvedere just above **Rifugio Perugia**, overlooking the Piano Grande to the south of Castelluccio (where there is parking), a good and fairly level 8-km walk winds around the contours of the mountains above the plain, passing through beech woods before ending either on a grassy spur of the mountain that juts north, or, if you feel like a short ascent, at the 1647-m summit. The views all along this route are stunning.

From the belvedere, follow the little-used road to the right that heads gently downhill toward the wood. Pass by ski lifts on your right before branching left along a path as the road descends to Piano Piccolo, another plain, to the right. Follow this path through small beech woods and along the sides of exceptionally steep grassy slopes high above the Piano Grande.

Alternatively, for a higher route, with views across the Piano Grande to the usually snow-capped Monte Vettore and Cima del Redentore, head northwest from the belvedere around the western edge of the plain below. This route, which can also be done by mountain bike, eventually takes you into Castelluccio.

❶ Directory

Spello *p58*
Hospital via Massimo Arcamone, Foligno, T0742-339 7408. **Pharmacy** Bartoli, via Cavour 63, T0742-301488.

Bevagna *p61*
Hospital via Massimo Arcamone, Foligno, T0742-339 7408.

Spoleto *p65, map p66*
Hospital via Loreto, T0743-210307.
Pharmacy Amici, piazza Giuseppe Garibaldi, T0743-46602.

Southwest Umbria

On a spectacular plug of volcanic rock rising like a huge wedding cake from the valley floor, Orvieto is a magnificent sight. And towering over the town is its biggest building: from miles away the cathedral dominates the landscape, its enormous façade covered with alarming depictions of sin and sinners. It's as near to Rome as to Perugia, and cosmopolitan weekenders have helped to keep an unusual number of good restaurants in business and give the town a less provincial feel than many places in Umbria. The local crisp white wine is another draw, and there are some interesting shops and a couple of good museums; you can also descend into the honeycomb of tunnels and wells dug into the tufa over the centuries.

Along a winding road to the northeast, Todi is another popular destination, at least in part for the self-perpetuating notion that it has the highest quality of life in the world. Whatever the truth in such a story, it's worth a visit for its beautiful piazza and the awesome engineering of the ancient Roman cisterns underneath.

To the south there is a prehistoric forest, beautiful Roman remains at Carsulae, and Narni, an under-visited hill town with alarming underground remains and a great museum.

Orvieto → *For listings, see pages 100-106.*

Orvieto's tufa plateau is an obvious place for a town, and it has been inhabited since Etruscan times, when the locals started the long tradition of boring down into the rock to make wine cellars, find water, throw away rubbish and hide the bodies of the dead. The enormous Duomo dominates the town and has some fantastic frescoes. Orvieto is also the centre of Umbrian wine making and there are many good places to test the blend. A handful of good museums, a tower and several ways to explore the subterranean history of the place make it an excellent place to visit, or indeed in which to base a stay in Umbria.

Arriving in Orvieto

Getting there Orvieto Scalo is on the main Rome to Florence line; you'll need to change to get to Perugia. With a car, it's also easy to reach Orvieto from Todi, though by public transport it's nearly impossible.

Getting around A funicular comes up the hill at the eastern end of town every 10 minutes from the car park and train station, arriving in piazza Cahen, from where you can walk anywhere. A 70-minute ticket costs €1 and is also valid on buses. A small electric bus, on which funicular tickets are valid, runs every few minutes from the top of the funicular to piazza del Duomo and back. Orvieto train station is in Orvieto Scalo, down in the valley.

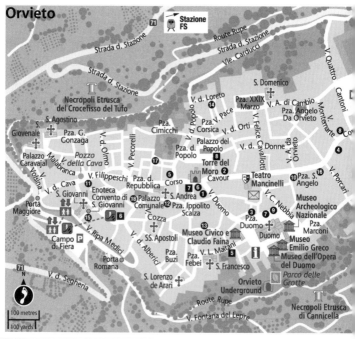

Tourist information Tourist information office ① *piazza del Duomo 24, T0763-344 1772, Mon-Fri 0815-1350, 1600-1900, Sat-Sun 1000-1300, 1500-1800.* There's also a seasonal office at the top of the funicular on piazza Cahen, but the one by the *duomo* is especially knowledgeable and has much more information. Orvieto's **Carta Unica** (www.cartaunica.it, €18, concession €15), gets you into nine sites/museums around town. It's valid for a year, so it may be worth it if you're going to be around for a while and plan on seeing a lot. Ask at the **Consorzio per la Tutela dei Vini DOC Orvieto e Rosso Orvietano** ① *corso Cavour 36, T0763-343790, www.consorziovinidiorvieto.it,* or at tourist information for details of local vineyards open to visitors.

Duomo
① *Daily Apr-Sep 0930-1900, Mar and Oct 0930-1800, Nov-Feb 0930-1300, 1430-1700, €3 (includes admission to Museo dell'Opera del Duomo and Museo Emilio Greco).*
Orvieto's grandest sight is its huge cathedral, towering over the town and the surrounding countryside. Inside is a mass of Gothic and Renaissance art as well as some impressive architecture. Outside are four famous panels illustrating the *Creation*, *David and Abraham*, the *Life of Jesus*, and *Heaven and Hell* in exquisite – and sometimes painful – detail. At sunset the façade is at its most impressive: the tallest building in the city, the *duomo* is also the last to catch the evening light.

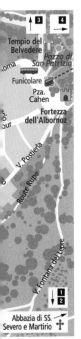

Where to stay 🛏
Il Libro d'Oro 1
Grand Hotel Reale 8
La Badia 2
Locanda Palazzone 3
Locanda Rosati 4
Maitani 5
Palazzo Piccolomini 6
Posta 7

Restaurants 🍴
Antico Bucchero 1
Barrique 2
Cantina Foresi 3
Cavour 222 4
Da Carlo 5
Dolceamaro 6
Enoteca Tozzi 7
Gelateria La Musa 8
Gelateria Pasqualetti 9
I Sette Consoli 10
Il Vincaffè 11
La Palomba 12
La Pergola 13
La Volpe e L'Uva 14
Le Grotte del Funaro 15
Pizzeria Charlie 16
Trattoria dell'Orso 17
Zeppelin 18

Cappella della Madonna di San Brizio
The most richly decorated walls of Orvieto's cathedral are extraordinary expanses of colour and nightmarish activity. The frescoes of the San Brizio Chapel appear so modern that in many ways they are nearer 20th-century graphic novels than traditional Renaissance style. As flying demons send down beams of fire, naked, muscle-bound figures writhe in agony, falling outside the frames of the picture. Meanwhile, tsunamis carry away ships, the moon turns red, the undead rise from their tombs and the world ends, while angels gaze calmly down from above.

Built between 1408 and 1444, the decoration of the chapel's vaults was planned and begun by Fra Angelico in 1447, but the main panels were not painted until 1499-1504, by Luca Signorelli. They depict *The Antichrist*, *The End of the World*, *The Resurrection of the Body*, *Hell*, *The Calling of the Chosen* and *Paradise*. Memorable, but deserving of an 18 certificate, Signorelli's images may have taken their lead from Dante, as well as from the bas-reliefs on the cathedral's façade. It's hard to believe that any Orvietans have dared to sin since.

Cappella del Corporale In the far left corner as you enter the cathedral, this chapel doesn't get the plaudits of its counterpart opposite, but perhaps deserves a little more recognition. Colourful frescoes from floor to ceiling illustrate the miracle of Bolsena in 1263 (when blood is said to have seeped from the Eucharist in the nearby town, confirming the doctrine of transubstantiation): the chapel was built to house the corporal, or linen cloth, on which the blood appeared. Lippo Memmi's *Madonna* is an especially beautiful and expressive painting. Elegant, poised and sensual, she stands looking out as angels above daintily pull back her cloak to reveal men and women below, their faces upturned in awe and hope.

Museo Claudio Faina

ⓘ *Piazza Faina 29, T0763-341511, www.museofaina.it, daily Apr-Sep 0930-1800, guided tours 1100 and 1600, Oct-Mar (Nov-Mar closed Mon) 1000-1700, guided tours 1100 and 1500, €4.50.*
Orvieto has a confusing plethora of different museums containing archaeological finds. The best is probably this one, opposite the *duomo*, named after the man who donated his family's collection. On the ground floor, the collection of the Museo Civico contains some great pieces from the nearby sacred Etruscan site of Cannicella. The stone statue of Venus, from around 530 BC, has been well worn by the passing millennia, but she retains an enigmatic smile. A huge stone warrior's head dates from the sixth century BC, and a wonderfully intact, and startlingly ugly, Gorgon's head is from the fifth century BC.

Upstairs, the Faina Collection includes some stunning Greek pots, including three beautiful amphorae by Exekias, a master of the genre, from the sixth century BC. Also here are some expressive funeral urns of the second century BC, with fighting figures below and wonderfully relaxed reclining depictions of the deceased on the lids. There is an extensive coin collection, and, on the second floor, some excellent bucchero pottery with a metallic sheen, made black by using ferric oxide and dating from as far back as the seventh century BC.

Museo Archeologico Nazionale

ⓘ *Palazzo Papale, piazza del Duomo, T0763-341039, www.archeopg.arti.beniculturali.it, daily 0830-1930, €3, combined ticket with Necropoli del Crocifisso del Tufo €5.*
Orvieto's second archeological museum has an extensive collection of Etruscan pottery, mostly organized according to the tombs in which it was found. The display is badly labelled and badly lit, but there are interesting pieces, including armour and a huge shield from the fourth century BC, and a four-headed, four-compartment pot from the same time that might have been used for condiments.

The best bits are the two recreated tombs with fourth-century-BC frescoes, fragmentary but fascinating. In one, a man plays a double flute and pomegranates form a part of the funeral feast.

Museo dell'Opera del Duomo

ⓘ *Piazza del Duomo 26, T0763-343592, www.opsm.it, Jan-Feb and Nov-Dec Wed-Mon 0930-1300, 1500-1700; Mar and Oct Wed-Mon 0930-1300, 1500-1800; Apr-Sep daily 0930-1900, €6.50, concessions €5.*
In effect several museums accessed with one ticket – it includes the Chiesa di Sant'Agostino and two picture galleries in piazza del Duomo – the Museo dell'Opera del Duomo is a disparate collection with some interesting highlights. The main museum, adjoining the *duomo*, holds a beautiful though strangely proportioned sculpture of the *Madonna and Child surrounded by angels* (1325), which once sat in the centre of the *duomo*'s façade. Attributed to Lorenzo Maitani, it is a wonderfully poised piece. There are several ornate

Simone Martini paintings from the early 14th century and a large, voluptuous *Santa Maria Maddalena* by Luca Signorelli, painted in 1504. What appears at first glance to be a self-portrait of Signorelli is almost certainly a 19th-century fake – the Latin on the back of the panel has many spelling mistakes and the wrong materials were used. By contrast to the medieval works, the huge 16th- to 18th-century panels in the other rooms are bombastic and uninteresting.

The **Museo Emilio Greco** is a rather more unlikely part of the *duomo* museum conglomerate. The Sicilian sculptor finished making the new doors of the cathedral in 1970, but this collection centres on his interest in the female body. Sketches and sculpture from the 1960s and 1970s are, at their best, seductive, though some have something of *The Joy of Sex* about them.

Orvieto Underground

① *Piazza del Duomo 23, T0763-340688, www.orvietounderground.it, daily tours at 1100, 1215, 1600, 1715 (weekends only in Feb), €6, concession €5.*

Built on a giant plug of volcanic stone, people have been tunnelling down into the rock below Orvieto for thousands of years. Guided tours (usually at least one a day in English) show a linked subterranean world of workplaces, secret passages and living spaces. As you enter the underground complex a map shows some 400 of the town's excavations, but even these are only a third of the estimated total. The tour includes a 40-m-deep Etruscan well, caves dug out for cement, networks of medieval dovecotes where pigeons were kept for food, and a 20th-century bomb shelter. At one time, when a tax was imposed on goods entering Orvieto, the town's underground network was even used for smuggling. The hour-long tour gives a novel and interesting insight into centuries of life here.

Torre del Moro

① *Corso Cavour 87, T0763-344567, daily May-Aug 1000-2000, Mar-Apr and Sep-Oct 1000-1900, Nov-Feb 1030-1300, 1430-1700, €3.*

The clock is a relatively recent addition, as are the modern stairs, but the tower itself dates from the 12th century. You can take a lift to the second floor, from where it's a long climb, via the back of the clock face, to the top. The 360° views make it well worth the effort, however.

Necropoli del Crocifisso del Tufo

① *Just outside the city walls, T0763-343611, www.archeopg.arti.beniculturali.it, daily Apr-Oct 0830-1930, Nov-Mar 0830-1730, €3, combined ticket with Museo Archeologico Nazionale €5.*

Dating from the sixth century BC, Orvieto's Etruscan necropolis is an impressive, even eerie place, where tombs constructed from massive square blocks of volcanic stone are lined up in rows at the bottom of the town's cliffs. Family names are carved on the lintels of the chambers, from where many of the finds in the town's museums were taken. You can wander freely among the dark, musty tombs, and down steps into many of them. A room at the entrance has a good display of information and a handful of finds from the necropolis.

Il Palazzo del Gusto

① *Via Ripa Serancia 16, T0763-341818, www.ilpalazzodelgusto.it, daily mid-Jun to mid-Sep 1100-1300, 1700-1900, mid-Sep to mid-Jun 1100-1300, 1500-1700.*

In a converted convent at the western edge of the city, the *enoteca* offers tours and wine-tasting in a great setting. The original Etruscan wine cellars have been added to and built over for centuries, and wine has been stored here for 2500 years. Exhibits in the cellars illustrate the importance of wine to Etruscan society, as well as to all societies here ever since. Above ground, the building has some fine cloisters, in the centre of which is a well built by Antonio da Sangallo, who also built the well of Pozzo di San Patrizio (see below). Other parts of the building, including the elegant conical tower, are being restored to allow more space for cookery and wine courses. The building is the centre of **Cittàslow**, an international organization trying to combat the homogenizing influences of fast food with an appreciation of local produce and traditions.

There are free tours (Monday-Friday) and wine-tasting too. If there are enough people, you may also be able to go on a tour at the weekend. You can, of course, also buy wine here, and for the really serious, professional sommelier courses are available.

Teatro Mancinello
ⓘ *Corso Cavour 122, T0763-340422, www.teatromancinelli.it, daily 1000-1300, 1500-1800, €2, concession €1.*
A small but grand 19th-century neoclassical theatre on the main street, ornately decorated. You can poke your head into a box, or wander up to the spacious 'foyer' where recitals are held. The theatre's season runs from October to March. Buy your tickets downstairs in the café, where you might also want to have a cup of one of their many teas.

Pozzo di San Patrizio
ⓘ *Viale Sangallo, off piazza Cahen, T0763-343768, May-Aug 0900-2000, Mar-Apr and Sep-Oct 0900-1900, Nov-Jan 1000-1700, €5, concession €3.50.*
This giant well was commissioned in 1527 by Pope Clement VII, who was worried that he might at some point have to take refuge in Orvieto. It took 10 years' digging to finally hit water. The structure hasn't changed since: two independent spiral staircases, big enough for a donkey to use, twist around the 53-m-deep and 13-m-wide hole cut into the rock. Each staircase (one for up, one for down) has 248 steps. Despite the 72 windows into the shaft it's fairly dark, and cool, which may be a blessing in summer.

Those who are less than generous in Italy are said to have 'pockets as deep as the Pozzo di San Patrizio'.

Pozzo della Cava
ⓘ *Via della Cava 28, T0763-342373, www.pozzodellacava.it, Tue-Sun 0900-2000, closed 2nd half of Jan, €3, concession €2.*
An Etruscan well at the western edge of town, Pozzo della Cava would be an impressive piece of engineering of any era. A wide circular shaft drops 25 m into the rock, with the water illuminated at the bottom. Unlike the Pozzo di San Patrizio, it's not possible to descend to the bottom, but it's satisfying to throw coins down – it's so far down that they start to whistle before they reach the water at the bottom. The square hole at the side is the original bore hole.

In typical Orvieto fashion, the holes in the rock here have been used for many different things over the years. For some time the well was used as a place to throw the bodies of miscreants, and there are other chutes here that were used to dispose of rubbish in medieval times. Other parts of the same complex were used as a necropolis and as a kiln, and once you've bought a ticket you'll go through an exhibition area filled with fragments of ancient ceramics found here. More recently, parts of these caves were used as air-raid shelters.

Route Rupe

Once you're in Orvieto, the tufa plateau on which it sits can easily be forgotten. But a path around the whole town threads through woods and around the base of the rock, giving great views to the west, especially at sunset. The whole circuit of the cave-threaded rock face is around 5 km. There are a few points around the edge of the city where you can join the path – see map for details.

Todi → *For listings, see pages 100-106.*

Atop a triangular hill in the River Tiber regional park, Todi has long been singled out as one of Umbria's most picturesque spots. Legends have it that the city was founded either by Hercules, or when an eagle stole a tablecloth from a tribe colonizing the area and dropped it on the top of the hill. The settlers took this as a divine command, and both the bird and the cloth can be seen in the town's emblem. In Etruscan times the town was called Tutere, meaning 'border', and it later became Roman Tuder. In the 13th century it captured local towns Amelia and Terni and several of its most impressive buildings were constructed.

Part of Todi's urban legend is that it is 'the world's most desirable place to live'. This conclusion, reached in the 1980s, was based more on marketing than rigorous research, but it has stuck. Consequently, the streets are full of English-speaking estate agents, and property prices have sky-rocketed out of the reach of most locals. The town also gets a disproportionate number of visitors, drawn by the beautiful medieval piazza, two much-lauded Renaissance churches, a good museum and some impressive Roman remains.

Arriving in Todi

Getting there Todi is on the regional Perugia to Terni line (www.umbriamobilita.it), with about nine trains a day from Perugia Santa Anna station (45 minutes). From Orvieto buses are so infrequent as to make the journey impractical, but from Perugia there are nine buses a day, taking one hour 15 minutes.

Getting around From the car park at viale Monedanto, outside Porta Orvietana, a lift takes you up into the *centro storico*. There is also free parking behind Santa Maria della Consolazione. There are buses from Perugia, but not all stop in the centre of Todi. The train station (Todi Ponte Rio) is about 3 km outside town, but a bus meets the trains.

Tourist information Tourist information office ⓘ *piazza del Popolo 38, T075-894 5416, Mar-Oct Mon-Sat 0930-1300, 1530-1830, Sun 1000-1300; Nov-Feb Mon-Sat 0930-1300, 1500-1800, Sun 1000-1300.*

Piazza del Popolo

With the *duomo* at one end and three 13th-century *palazzi* around it, piazza del Popolo is a fine, well-preserved, medieval square. On the site of the ancient Roman forum, it also sits on top of the huge Roman cisterns (see below). The most striking of the piazza's buildings are the conjoined pair of **Palazzo del Popolo** and **Palazzo del Capitano**, housing the town's museum and art gallery. Palazzo del Popolo, on the corner of piazza Garibaldi, was begun in 1213, and is the older of the two. Work on its neighbour, with its grand staircase, was started 27 years later. **Palazzo dei Priori**, facing the *duomo*, was begun in 1293. It has an unusual trapezoidal tower and a 14th-century bronze eagle.

Museo Civico e Pinacoteca

ⓘ *Piazza del Popolo, T075-895 6216, Apr-Oct Tue-Sun 1000-1330, 1500-1800, Nov-Mar Tue-Sun 1030-1300, 1430-1700, €3.50.*

The town's museum and picture gallery is worth a visit for its ancient pre-Roman and Roman remains and for some of its large paintings. Downstairs there are Etruscan bronze candlesticks and slingshot, and a 12th-century fragment depicting a cheerily waving Jesus with two of Todi's patron saints, Fortunato and Cassiano. A scale model of Santa Maria della Consolazione enables you to see how the building was designed, and there are relic holders, some complete with fragments of arms, teeth and so on. The Roman section has a nicely quizzical pair of doves and a bronze pig looking very well fattened.

In the picture gallery, the highlights are paintings by Lo Spagna, especially a large, colourful *Coronation of the Virgin* from 1511. Also here is a much smaller painting of *Beato Bernardino da Feltre* by the same artist from 1515.

Look out too for interesting temporary archaeological and art exhibitions in the **Sala delle Pietre**, a large room on the first floor of the palazzo.

Cisterne Romane

ⓘ *Via del Monte, T075-894 4148, Apr-Oct Tue-Sun 1000-1330, 1500-1800, Nov-Mar, Sat-Sun 1030-1300, 1430-1700, €2.*

An extraordinary feat of engineering in any age, Todi's dripping Roman cisterns, right below the centre of the city, are one of the region's more impressive Roman remains. Huge, atmospheric spaces, the part open to the public is merely a fraction of a complex underground network of galleries and tunnels, stretching for 5 km through the hill under Todi. This section was discovered only in 1996, during work on a shop above. The shop in question – a *tabacchi* in the piazza – has a glass floor through which you can see the remains below. Though there were local stories of a massive underground lake here, they were not widely believed until the cistern was discovered. It is 48 m long and 6.7 m high. Another cistern, on the other side of the piazza, has been known about since 1262. When full, each chamber would have held around 2500 cu m of water. During Todi's annual arts festival, the cistern is sometimes used as an atmospheric venue for video art.

Duomo

ⓘ *Piazza del Popolo, daily 0830-1230, 1430-1830, free, crypt €1.*

At the northern end of piazza del Popolo, Todi's cathedral has an impressive carved portal on a pale pink, square façade, below a large rose window. There are two smaller rose windows above the two side doors. Building commenced in the 12th century and continued for centuries thereafter. The steps at the front – a good place to sit and watch the goings-on in the piazza – were added in the 18th century. Go down the road to the right of the cathedral to see the ornate side of the building. Inside, the choir is an intricate work of carving by a father and son in the early 16th century. In the crypt various pieces from the cathedral's treasury are on display, including three 13th-century statues from the Pisano school.

Tempio di San Fortunato

ⓘ *Piazza Umberto I, T075-894 5311, campanile Apr-Oct Tue-Sun 1000-1300, 1500-1830, Nov-Mar Tue-Sun 1030-1300, 1430-1700, €1.50.*

Tall and light, with elegant columns, the Church of San Fortunato overlooks the steep slope of the town's second piazza. The upper part of the façade is unfinished, though the lower half makes up for this with an ornately decorated portal with exquisitely carved leaves and figures.

Inside, Masolino's *Madonna and Child*, in the fourth chapel on the left, is a beautiful painting with pretty angels on either side of the Virgin. In the apse, the statue of St Fortunato is from 1643; note the eagle with tablecloth below. Climb the 150 steps to the top of the *campanile*, popular with pigeons, for good views of the town and the surrounding countryside below.

In the crypt is the **tomb of Jacopone da Todi** (1228-1306), one of Italy's most famous medieval poets. At the age of 40, Jacopone's wife died in an accident; when he discovered that, unbeknown to him, she had been wearing a hair shirt, he gave up his comfortable existence and lived a life of penitence and poverty, wandering the countryside and writing poetry that was often acerbically critical of the church and its excesses and corruption.

Teatro Comunale
① *Via Mazzini, T075-895 6700.*
If there's anything on at the sumptuous Teatro Comunale while you're in Todi, you may be able to wander in to this beautiful, oval, four-tiered theatre during the day to have a quick look round, or you could book seats in a box and go to see the production. The theatre was built in 1872 by Carlo Gatteschi and holds up to 500 people.

Parco della Rocca
① *Apr-Oct 0630-2200, Nov-Mar 0700-1900.*
At the highest point in the city, with views to the south, the Parco dell Rocca is a pleasant place for a wander among the roses and the shade of the trees. The tower known as 'il Mastio' is all that remains of the fortifications, built here by Pope Gregory XI in 1373.

Tempio di Santa Maria della Consolazione
① *Wed-Mon, Apr-Oct 0900-1300, 1430-1800, Nov-Mar 1000-1230, 1430-1800, free.*
A masterpiece of Renaissance architecture, the light, airy and open Santa Maria della Consolazione was probably built to a design by Donato Bramante, who also designed St Peter's in Rome. Work on the church began in 1508, and it was eventually completed 99 years later. It stands outside the city walls: you can climb down a long set of stairs from the Parco della Rocca to reach it. It has a central dome surrounded by four half-domes, as if two domes have been slid apart to allow space for another. Sixty enormous rose bosses, many with rather scary mythological creatures in their centres, line the arches.

Ab Ovo Gallery
① *Via del Forno 4, T075-894 5526, www.abovogallery.com, Mar-mid to Jan Tue-Sun 1030-1330, 1530-1930, free.*
A sophisticated, high-end craft gallery, Ab Ovo was set up in Todi's medieval bakery by an Italian/English partnership and exhibits delicate pieces of fine ceramics, jewellery, furniture and even bags, made by international artists. The pieces are carefully curated, and group shows, often loosely themed, are rotated about three times a year. Nothing here is cheap, but it may just be worth saving up for.

Foresta Fossile di Dunarobba

① *Vocabolo Pennicchia 46, Dunarobba, Avigliano Umbro, 17 km south of Todi on SP379, T0744-940348, www.forestafossile.it, Jul-Aug Tue-Sun 1000-1300, 1630-1930; rest of summer (coinciding with the changing of the clocks) Tue-Fri 1000-1300, Sat-Sun 1000-1300, 1630-1930; winter Tue-Fri 1000-1300, Sat-Sun 1000-1300, 1400-1600, €5, concession €3.*

Discovered in a clay quarry near the town of Avigliano Umbro in the late 1970s, the huge trees of Dunarobba are 1.5 million years old. Despite the name, these prehistoric trees are not actually fossils at all – the wood was simply preserved, mummified in clay, and it still looks like fresh timber. The trees were a type of giant sequoia and though only stumps remain, some are 5-10 m high and 1.5 m in diameter.

Narni → *For listings, see pages 100-106.*

At the precise geographical centre of Italy, Narni is a place strangely unaccustomed to visitors, despite being a hilltop town of some beauty and having some excellent attractions. The town's underground tour is fascinating, there are some attractive Romanesque churches and a fantastic new museum and art gallery. It can require a little effort, however – some of its best sights are open only at weekends, and tourist information is decidedly unhelpful. The Umbrian town of Nequinium was renamed Narnia (after the River Nar) by the Romans when they conquered the town in 299 BC. CS Lewis quite possibly named his magical kingdom after it, but links to stone lions around the town are almost certainly fanciful.

Nearby, sleepy Amelia is a beautiful town at the centre of the Amerino area. In the other direction, Carsulae, on the via Flaminia, is one of the most complete Roman remains in Italy and sits in a stunning location under wooded hills.

Arriving in Narni

Getting there There are direct trains from Spoleto to Narni-Amelia (35 minutes). Buses (www.umbriamobilita.it) run from Amelia (15 or so a day, around 30 minutes) and there are about five a day from Orvieto (around 75 minutes).

Getting around You can park in piazza Garibaldi. Buses run from piazza Garibaldi to the centre. The train station, known as Narni-Amelia, is in Narni Scalo, about 4 km to the north of the centre of Narni. Buses run from here to town.

Tourist information Tourist information office ① *Pro Loco Narni, piazza dei Priori 3, T0744-715362, Tue-Sun 0930-1230, 1700-1900.* Not Umbria's most helpful tourist office.

Narni Sotterranea

① *Via San Bernardo 12, T0744-722292, www.narnisotterranea.it, visits by guided tour only, Apr-Oct Sat 1500 and 1800, Sun and holidays 1000, 1115, 1230, 1500, 1615, 1730, Nov-Mar Sun and holidays 1100, 1215, 1500, 1615, €6.*

Narni's underground wonders were discovered in 1979 by a group of young speleologists. Despite the fact that they had just shimmied down a rock face on to his lettuces, an old gardener showed them a small hole in the ground in the corner of his plot. That hole has now been widened into a doorway and leads into a 12th-century church, which was used as a wine cellar by Napoleonic troops and subsequently forgotten about. Frescoes, also from the 12th century, show the coronation of the Virgin and two depictions of St Michael, to whom the church is dedicated. Stars on a blue ceiling can be made out, as well as some human bones buried under the floor.

The second room they discovered was a Roman cistern, and here are some displays and recreations of surveying tools the Romans used to build their nearby aqueduct, which featured a tunnel that was started from both ends and met in the middle. This tunnel can also be visited if you book in advance.

Beyond the cistern is a room that was used by the Inquisition as a torture chamber, complete with some tools of the trade. Most intriguing, though, is the cell off this room, which is covered in carved graffiti. Most of this was done in 1759 by someone called Giuseppe Lombardini, a guard-turned-prisoner, when he was imprisoned on suspicion of helping somebody to escape. Full of Masonic and religious symbolism, it is a fascinating riddle as well as an insight into the mind of someone trapped down here. In 2008 a Byzantine mosaic was found under the floor of the Church of San Domenico, above.

Led by one of the original speleologists, Narni Sotterranea tours are conducted (in English as well as Italian) with a rare enthusiasm, as well as plenty of humour and knowledge.

Museo della Città di Narni

ⓘ *Palazzo Eroli, via Aurelio Saffi, T0744-717117, www.museoeroli.it, Apr-Jun and Sep Tue-Sun 1030-1300, 1530-1800, Jul-Aug Tue-Sun 1030-1300, 1630-1930, Oct-Mar Fri-Sun 1030-1300, 1500-1730, €5, concession €3.*

Narni's excellent museum and art gallery is a two-for-one bargain. In the Palazzo Eroli, an ancient stone lion, purportedly used by CS Lewis as a model for Aslan, greets visitors. Upstairs, on the first floor, a huge pair of mammoth's tusks precedes a collection of mainly Roman remains. These are excellently displayed – there is no overload of pieces and the well-chosen finds are attractively lit, though for the moment the information is only in Italian. Audioguides in English are planned. Look out especially for the Roman carved stone sarcophagus of the family Latuedi, with three portraits of son, father and mother. There are also some good medieval pieces – an eighth- or ninth-century altar from San Martino di Taizzano has some beautiful carvings, and there are some wonderfully expressive carvings from the 12th and 13th centuries, especially two men with shields and a man with a griffin. The original 14th-century basin from the town's Piazza Garibaldi fountain is also here.

In the second-floor picture gallery, the star is without doubt Domenico Ghirlandaio's 1486 *Coronation of the Virgin*. Before you reach this there are a few beautiful pieces from the early 14th century, such as a two-sided panel depicting the Madonna: one with child, one at her coronation. Ghirlandaio's masterpiece is in its own room. Black walls make it feel a little like entering a cinema, and there is always a guide on hand to give a description of the painting, together with spotlights that cleverly isolate parts of the work. Adding to the sense of drama, Baroque music plays – only instruments found in the painting were used.

The contrast between the stylized expression of the preceding art and Ghirlandaio's detailed and dazzling, almost photographic, precision is marked. On earth below, St Francis and his associates look up to heaven above, where the Virgin is crowned, surrounded by prophets. Every face here is remarkably human, and the fabrics also show virtuoso skill. On the upper level, representing heaven, one woman stands out among the assembled men, and it has been surmised that she must have been somebody important to the artist, though her identity remains a mystery.

Gozzoli's *Annunciation* is another highlight – at the time of writing it is being restored, but it is hoped that it will be back on display in the museum soon. A café, beyond the bookshop, has great views over the valley.

Cattedrale San Giovenale
ⓘ *Piazza Cavour, daily, approximately 0900-1330, 1600-1800.*
Overlooking both piazza Cavour and piazza Garibaldi, Narni's cathedral was consecrated in 1145. It has 12th-century decoration around its main door, and a portico that was added later, in the 15th century. Inside there are some ancient treasures among the strangely mixed design. The Oratorio of San Cassio, on the right-hand wall, is a small chapel built in the sixth century around the grave of the town's first bishop. The wizened remains of Beata Lucia (probably unconnected to CS Lewis's Lucy, despite many claims to the contrary) are behind glass further along the same side.

Rocca di Albornoz
ⓘ *Information at the museum, Palazzo Eroli, T0744-717117, visits by guided tour only, Apr-May Fri-Sun 1100-1300, 1500-1800, Jun-Jul Sat-Sun 1100-1300, 1500-1800, Aug-Sep daily 1100-1300, 1600-1900, Oct-Mar Sat-Sun 1100-1300, 1500-1700, €3, under 12s free.*
High above Narni is one of a chain of fortresses erected by Cardinal Albornoz in Umbria to reinforce papal rule. Built between 1360 and 1378, and restored and reinforced many times since, it has a quadrilateral form with towers on its corners. To reach it follow via XX Settembre from piazza Garibaldi – it's about a 15-minute walk.

The rest of the town
Two medieval buildings, **Palazzo dei Priori** and **Palazzo del Podestà**, face each other across the administrative centre of town, the piazza dei Priori. The former was designed by Umbrian architect Gattapone in the 14th century. The road running north and south from here was the original *cardo maximus* of the Roman town.

Narni has several interesting churches, including the beautiful little 12th-century Romanesque **Church of Santa Maria Impensole** ⓘ *via Mazzini, just north of piazza dei Priori, daily approximately 0900-1300, 1600-1830*, which has a beautiful triple-arched portico and two worn griffins guarding the door. Inside, look for the carved capitals on the columns.

Remnants of Roman Narnia in and around piazza Garibaldi include an arch and a gate in the city walls just to the west. An underground cistern (steps in the centre of Piazza Garibaldi lead down to a barred door with an easily missed light switch to the right) dates from the early Middle Ages and was fed by a Roman aqueduct.

Amelia

Half an hour's drive west of Narni is the sleepy hill town of Amelia, with ancient walls built around the fifth century BC. Parts have been reconstructed since, but other sections, consisting of huge blocks of stone, remain. According to Roman historian Pliny, the town may have been founded as early as 800 BC, before Rome itself.

Inside the walls is a town where not very much changes very quickly. There's the **Museo Archeologico** ⓘ *piazza Augusto Vera, T0744-978120, Oct-Mar Fri-Sun 1030-1300, 1530-1800, Apr-May, Jun and Sep 1030-1300, 1600-1900, Jul-Aug 1030-1300, 1630-1930, €5*, with some interesting pieces. At the top of the town, next to the cathedral, stands a 12-sided clock tower, the **Torre Civico**, which dates back to 1050 – the date is inscribed on one of the stones at the base.

Otherwise Amelia is a pretty but not overly prettified town, a place to gently wander and appreciate the light shining through old arches, cats sleeping on battered stone steps and some dusty old antique shops. It's also known for its fig-candied-orange-and-chocolate *fichi girotti*.

Carsulae

ⓘ *19 km north of Narni, T0744-334133, www.carsulae.it, 22 Mar-25 Oct 0830-1930, 26 Oct-21 Mar 0830-1730, €5, concession €3.50, off SS3bis (take the turning for Fonti di San Gemini and follow signs for about 3 km).*

Umbria's most complete Roman remains are in one of the region's most stunning locations, under thickly wooded hills. Not much more than a stopping post on the via Flaminia, little was written about the town in Roman times. And, in terms of spectacular architecture, Carsulae cannot compete with Pompeii or Paestum further south. Where it excels, however, is in summoning up the atmosphere of ancient times. Once you've left the ticket office and passed through the turnstiles, there's almost nothing to remind you of the 2000 years that have passed since Carsulae was a thriving Roman town. As the via Flaminia passes through oak trees on its way to the **Arco di Traiano** (also known as the Arco di San Damiano), complete with grooves ground into the stone by ancient carriage wheels, it is easy to imagine that around the corner might be centurions returning home.

After the via Flaminia was rerouted through Interamna (Terni) and Spoletium (Spoleto) to the east, Carsulae was abandoned. Only the fourth- or fifth-century **Church of San Damiano**, in the middle of the site, was subsequently built here, using stones from the Roman ruins around it. Now restored, the church has some fragmentary 15th-century frescoes.

As well as the road itself, and the 8-m-high arch (once the centre of a three-arched entrance to the town), Carsulae has both a theatre and an amphitheatre in a single entertainment complex at the edge of the site, a temple, a basilica and a forum. Pick up a map of the site at the ticket office.

Southwest Umbria listings

For hotel and restaurant price codes and other relevant information, see pages 11-15.

🛏 Where to stay

Orvieto *p88, map p88*

€€€€ **La Badia**, località La Badia 8, T0763-301959, www.labadiahotel.it. Set among peaceful olive groves south of Orvieto on the road to Bagnoregio, the 12-sided tower of this 6th-century ex-abbey can easily be seen from the edge of the town. It's a fantastic location, and there's a good restaurant too, though the rooms and suites can feel dated. The public rooms, including a slick modern bar, are pristinely contemporary, however, and there's a swimming pool in summer.

€€€€ **Locanda Palazzone**, località Rocca Ripesena, near Sferracavallo, 4 km northwest of Orvieto, T0763-393614, www.locandapalazzone.com. A handsome medieval country house, this was a resting place for 14th-century pilgrims on their way to Rome. These days it has gone upmarket a little and has elegant contemporary suites, a swimming pool and views of Orvieto. It's a wine estate, and the house is surrounded by vineyards. Staff will suggest good local walks.

€€€ **Hotel Maitani**, via Lorenzo Maitani 5, T0763-342011, www.hotelmaitani.com. A short distance along the street opposite the cathedral, **Maitani** is steadfastly old-fashioned, for those who like their hotels buttoned up. The 39 rooms have baths and early 20th-century furniture and chandeliers, and there's a bar and a big lounge. Formal and (mostly) stylish.

€€€ **Palazzo Piccolomini**, piazza Ranieri 36, T0763-341743, www.palazzopiccolomini.it. Faultlessly friendly and professional, **Piccolimini** is an excellent option in the heart of Orvieto. The 34 rooms and suites have sturdy wooden furniture and a good range of mod cons, such as satellite TV

and minibars. The building dates back to the 15th century but the hotel feels modern, with nicely renovated rooms and big common spaces that use the original structure. Plentiful parking.

€€€-€€ **Grand Hotel Reale**, piazza del Popolo 25, T0763-341247. Growing old gracefully, the **Grand Hotel Reale** is a rare find: a stylishly antique pile that has had next to no gentrification. It may have occasional rough edges, but when you're staying in a frescoed room where King Umberto I slept in 1900, you can put up with those. There's a private chapel, some baths are solid marble, others are rolltop cast iron, and even the TVs are ancient. The stairs are wide enough to herd elephants up, and homely old leather furniture and plants decorate the place. The smallest, plainer rooms here are some of the cheapest in town.

€€ **Hotel Posta**, via Luca Signorelli 18, T0763-341909, www.orvietohotels.it. Big, cool, marble-floored rooms overlook a central garden. Not all rooms are en suite – those that are have bathrooms with lots of corners. There's a new lift, but otherwise not much to show for the rather slow renovation that has been going on for a while; hopefully when it's finished it won't detract from the stylish old-fashioned nature of the place. Friendly and good value.

€€ **Il Libro d'Oro**, località Botto, Canale, 6 km south of Orvieto, T340-948 9628, www.librodoro.net. Good-value apartments that can be rented on a B&B basis or used for self-catering. Rooms feature iron-framed beds, pale sofas, terracotta tiles, bare wood and views over the surrounding countryside. Shiatsu massage and meditation are available.

€€ **Locanda Rosati**, località Buonviaggio 22, T0763-217314, www.locandarosati.it. In a rural spot a few kilometres west of Orvieto, communal meals are a popular aspect of a stay at this stone country house with a swimming pool and verdant gardens.

Todi p93

For somewhere with so many visitors, Todi has a shortage of good accommodation in the town centre, though there are some good options in the surrounding hills.

€€€€ **Fattoria di Vibio**, località Buchella 9, Doglio, Montecastello di Vibio, 15 km north of Todi, T075-874 9607, www.fattoriadivibio.com. A large and well-equipped rural hotel with contemporary touches. Rustic style predominates – rooms are simple, with tiles and floral fabrics, but there's a less expected modern edge in the use of plate glass and steel in the spa. Separate cottages in the grounds (available by the week, from €1260), packages for romantic weekends, cookery courses and horse riding are all available.

€€€€ **Relais Todini**, Frazione Collevalenza, 9 km south of Todi, T075-887521, www.relaistodini.com. This handsome country house on a hill has 12 rooms, with frescoed walls, tapestries and antiques. There's a spa, a good pool and a wine cellar well stocked with wines from the surrounding vineyards.

€€€ **Fonte Cesia**, via Lorenzo Leonj 3, T075-894 3737, www.fontecesia.it. A stone's throw from piazza Umberto I, in the heart of Todi, **Fonte Cesia** just about has a monopoly over guests who want a *centro storico* hotel. Rooms are elegant, in a slightly old-fashioned way, with lots of frills and drapes, and are well equipped, with radios, a/c, satellite television, safes and minibars. There are 37 rooms and suites altogether; the latter are both more spacious and more stylish. Some also have balconies.

€€ **San Lorenzo Tre**, via San Lorenzo 3, T075-894 4555, www.sanlorenzo3.it. San Lorenzo sets itself apart from the average old-fashioned hotel by making almost everything exactly as it would have been 100 years ago. With the one concession to modernity of en suite bathrooms, this little place is genuinely antique. On the upper floor of a 17th-century house, it offers 6 rooms with elegant old furniture, 19th-century fabric designs, yellowing old pictures, and a definite absence of telephones and televisions. The best rooms have views over the countryside, and the whole place has a worn elegance and a charmingly homely feel.

Self-catering

Casa Menicaglie, midway between Todi and Orvieto, 3 km from Civitella del Lago, T+44 (0)7687-970458, carolyn@carolynlyons.co.uk. Owned by 2 English writers, **Casa Menicaglie** is a pretty hideaway in the hills above Lago di Corbara in the Parco Regionale del Tevere. Sleeping 5 and available by the week (£850), it's hard not to feel instantly at home here. Books line the walls and there's an attractive open kitchen and sitting area. Sit on the patio by the olive grove and watch the sun set behind Orvieto and the wooded hills above the Tiber Valley. At the end of the summer there are more figs than you could possibly eat, and probably the only sounds will be crickets and the occasional distant tractor, though you may hear the rustle of porcupines and wild boar at night.

Narni p96

€€€ **Hotel Minareto**, via dei Cappuccini Nuovi 32, T0744-760207. An ex-convent with great views, the hotel has a pool and refined rooms with metal-framed beds and a profusion of burgundy. There's not much evidence left of the Capuchin monks, however, bar some old walls and a couple of ancient pillars in what was once the cloister.

€€€ **Torre Palombara**, strada della Cantinetta 3, 6 km south of Narni, T0744-744617, www.torrepalombara.com. A country villa built around a 15th-century tower, with views of Narni. It's a quiet, elegant spot, with a pool and gardens. A sympathetic restoration, natural tones, wood and bare stonework are used to good effect, and cable TV and internet access are some of the modern comforts.

€€ **La Loggia dei Priori**, vicolo del Comune 4, T0744-726843, www.loggiadeipriori.it. A good 3-star in the centre of Narni,

Gelaterie

Orvieto has three great ice cream places, making it the best town in Umbria for a *gelato* – you should really try them all. **Dolceamaro**, corso Cavour 78, T0763-342125. A small selection of home-made ice cream and mouth-wateringly good chocolates, plus cakes and biscuits.

Gelateria La Musa, corso Cavour 351, T0763-393861. Fabulous home-made ice cream, including some unusual seasonal flavours, such as pears in Barolo wine. **Gelateria Pasqualetti**, piazza del Duomo 14, T0763-341034. Exquisite home-made ice cream opposite the *duomo*. Try the wild strawberry or the pink grapefruit.

dei Priori has 19 plain rooms and suites but cosy public spaces, with a greenery-draped courtyard and an open fire in winter. Some brick vaulting gives an element of medieval styling, and the welcome is friendly.

🍴 Restaurants

Orvieto *p88, map p88*

€€€€ I Sette Consoli, piazza Sant'Angelo 1a, T0763-343911, www.isetteconsoli.it. Thu-Tue 1230-1500, 1930-2200, closed Feb. Orvieto's smartest restaurant, I Sette Consoli is a barrel-vaulted place with a garden adorned with lots of white drapes. There's a €42 set menu featuring dishes such as spaghetti with rabbit and braised veal cheek.

€€€ Antico Bucchero, via de' Cartari 4, T0763-341725. Thu-Tue 1200 onwards, 1900 onwards. Tables outside in a beautiful little piazza, hidden away from most of the throng, are the biggest draw here, though the food is also excellent. Try the succulent melon and ham, and the excellent tortelloni filled with ricotta and radicchio with courgettes and pecorino.

€€€ Cavour 222, corso Cavour 222, T0763-393518. Tue-Sun 1200-1600, 1900-2200. A simple *osteria* halfway along the main street, with 5 tables outside under umbrellas. There are daily specials and good pasta with porcini. Nothing complicated, but a good spot for a late lunch with a view – they serve until 1600.

€€€ Da Carlo, vicolo del Popolo 9, T0763-344406. Tue-Sun. Unusually in Orvieto,

Da Carlo, on a quiet, pretty little piazza off corso Cavour, has a slick, young feel, with baby blue and white paintwork and bare wood. A handwritten blackboard menu changes regularly, but dishes may include sausage with grapes, pigeon with figs, or a spicy *pollo al rabbioncino*.

€€€ La Pergola, via dei Magoni 9b, T0763-343065. Thu-Tue 0900-1600, 1900-2400. Popular with locals, this little restaurant has a pretty garden at the back and serves good, unpretentious Umbrian food such as beef carpaccio with rocket and Parmesan, and gnocchi with spinach and truffle. The wine list also features some interesting artisan beers.

€€€ La Volpe e l'Uva, via Ripa Corsica 11, T0763-341612. Wed-Sun 1300-1500, 2000-2230. With small rooms under barrel-vaulted brick ceilings and white walls, this is a friendly place where the chef may well come out to chat. The back room has a/c and old, fading pictures. The handwritten menu is truffle-heavy, but you could also try the Lake Bolsena fish in white wine, and be sure to save some room for the excellent home-made biscuits with dessert wine.

€€€ Le Grotte del Funaro, via Ripa Serancia 41, T0763-343276, www.grottedel funaro.it. Tue-Sun 1200-1500, 1900-2400. Sit in cool, underground vaulted caves, once home to Orvieto's rope makers, or at tables outside, on the edge of the town with great views. Fish features nearly as much as meat on the menu, and there are 24 pizzas on offer too.

€€€ Trattoria dell'Orso, via della Misericordia 18-20, T0763-341642. Tue-Sat 1230-1400, 1930-2130. One of the oldest restaurants in town, Gabriele and Ciro's place is frequented by a cross-section of Orvieto – expect to eat here next to Italian aristocrats, businessmen, market stallholders and a few in-the-know visitors. All come for the simple but expertly prepared Umbrian food with a healthy side order of friendly patter. Prices are slightly higher than in the average trattoria, and the printed menu is almost completely ignored, but the owners speak good English and if you're happy to go with their recommendations you'll be guaranteed a fabulous meal of dishes such as pancakes stuffed with spinach and ricotta, chicken with peppers, or bass with courgettes. There's plenty of character in the 2 rooms – one yellow and red, one yellow and green – with an eclectic and colourful art collection and a Michelangeli wooden frieze.

€€€ Zeppelin, via Garibaldi 28, T0763-341447, www.ristorantezeppelin.it. Tue-Sun 1230-1430, 1930-2200. A big place with high, arched ceilings, **Zeppelin** has a marble bar, a garden with lemon trees and a menu with lots of exclamation marks and several set options, including a vegetarian menu and some carefully seasoned meaty choices. As well as eating, you can also cook here. 1-day courses focus on fresh pasta, poultry and game, truffles or vegetarian cuisine, or there's a half-day chocolate course.

€€ La Palomba, via Cipriano Manente 16, off piazza della Repubblica, T0763-343395. Thu-Tue 1230-1415, 1930-2200. A local place with wood panelling and photos old and new on the walls, serving traditional Umbrian dishes with few concessions to modernity – pigeon, tripe, lamb and boar all feature. Very reasonable prices.

€€ Pizzeria Charlie, corso Cavour 194, T0763-344766, www.pizzeriacharlieorvieto.it. Wed-Mon 1900-2330. Orvieto's best pizzas are served in this popular spot with small wooden tables inside and out on the main drag. There's German Paulaner beer on tap,

free Wi-Fi to accompany your Margherita, and – unusually for Orvieto – it stays open late into the evening.

Cafés and bars
Barrique, corso Cavour 111, T0763-340455. Tue-Sun 0700-2200. A good spot for people watching, **Barrique** does fantastic coffee and pretty good cakes too, and has tables outside on the street.

Cantina Foresi, piazza del Duomo 2, T0763-341611. Daily 1100-1930. On the piazza, with tables facing the *duomo*, this is a great spot for an *aperitivo* or a light meal – opt for a standard plate of meat and cheese or a more adventurous mixed selection of wild boar or pheasant with mushrooms.

Enoteca Tozzi, piazza del Duomo 13, T0763-344393. Daily 0900-2000. 2 tables outside face the side of the cathedral; inside is an unexpectedly high-ceilinged place with lots of wine and decent sandwiches for €2-3.

Il Vincaffè, via Filippeschi 39, T0763-340099, www.ilvincaffe.it. Wed-Fri 1230-1530, 1830-0200, Sat and Mon-Tue 1830-0200, Sun 1730-0200. An *enoteca* that stays open late and has unusually good vegetarian options such as courgette, lemon and ricotta salad, or lentils and pepper. It's a fairly simple place, with a bar, square wooden tables and jazz playing.

Todi *p93*
€€€ Antica Osteria della Valle, via Ciuffelli 17-21, T075-894 4848. Thu-Tue 1230-1430, 1930-2200. Seduced by Umbrian ingredients, the English chef of the **Antica Osteria della Valle** gave up working in restaurants in London to set up on his own here. Overcoming initial scepticism on the part of locals, it is now considered by many to be Todi's best restaurant. The seasonal menu always includes fish and a handful of signature dishes, such as ravioli with ricotta, spinach and cream of truffle. The restaurant also shows paintings from local artists, which change every few months.

€€€ Pane e Vino, via Ciuffelli 33, T075-894 5448, www.panevinotodi.com. Thu-Tue 1100-1530, 1830-2300. A simple but popular little place just off the street, with a few crowded tables outside and a 3-level, yellow-walled interior. Traditional Umbrian dishes predominate – the risotto with courgettes and saffron is rich and creamy, and the pasta with fresh tomatoes and lemons has a good tang to it. The mixed *crostini* are excellent too, and hunks of meat are enormous. Friendly service and extras such as warm home-made bread help attract both locals and visitors.

€€€ Ristorante Umbria, via San Bonaventura 13, T075-894 2737, www. ristoranteumbria.it. Wed-Mon 1230-1430, 1930-2230. Under the arches of Palazzo del Popolo, **Umbria** is a traditional restaurant with an open fire, over which meat is grilled, and a good self-service buffet of vegetables. It is best known for its terrace, however, which has enormous views over the surrounding countryside. Steadfastly Umbrian, truffles are joined on the menu by other local ingredients such as venison and chestnuts. Not a place to come if you're in a hurry, but a great spot to linger.

€€ Cavour, corso Cavour 21-23, T075-894 2491, www.ristorantecavour-todi.com. Thu-Tue 1200-1600, 1900-late. A large and good-value pizzeria, with an equally big choice of toppings, **Cavour** also has traditional dishes, and there's a bar with beer on tap. The brick-vaulted interior has slightly garish pink walls.

Cafés and bars

Enoteca Oberdan, via Ciuffelli 22, T075-894 5409. Wed-Sun 1200-2400. An attractive and laid-back wine bar, **Oberdan** offers a good selection of cheeses and cold meats as well as more substantial dishes such as spelt flour pasta with an aubergine, pepper and ricotta sauce. Wine is the mainstay, however, and bottles line the walls, around small square wooden tables and painted wooden chairs.

Pianegiani, corso Cavour 40, T075-894 2376, www.barpianegiani.it. Apr-Oct daily 0700-0100, Nov-Mar Sun-Fri 0700-2300. A fairly nondescript bar, **Pianegiani** does unexpectedly good ice cream, using good, local, seasonal ingredients.

Narni *p96*

€€€ Il Gattamelata, via Pozzo della Comunitá 4, T0744-717245. Tue-Sun around 1200 onwards, 1900 onwards. Overlooking the piazza Garibaldi, **Gattamelata** has a distinctive portico with good views. The menu has vegetarian suggestions as well as traditional local dishes such as *manfricoli* pasta or gnocchi with almonds, spinach and Parmesan, or you can go for a 'thin' or 'fat' medieval fixed menu featuring goose and eel, by reservation only.

€€€ Il Pincio, via XX Settembre 117, T0744-722241. Thu-Tue 1230-1500, 1930-2200. Stylish traditional Umbrian food with the addition of seafood on Tue, Thu and Fri. Part of the interior of the restaurant is a cave. Themed fixed menus through the year for around €45 are real feasts.

€€€ La Gallina Liberata, vicolo Belvedere 13, T0744-081561. Wed-Sun, lunch only (evenings by reservation). At first glance the 'Liberated Chicken' is a deceptively simple place, with 3 tables outside on a sandy, slightly decrepit stepped street. Inside it's much smarter: barrel vaulted, with a contemporary, flowing, painted design suggestive of the beach and sea. The fresh, home-made pasta dishes are some of the best you'll eat anywhere. The home-made desserts are also spectacular. A short, handwritten menu changes monthly.

€€ Terra & Arte, vicolo Belvedere 1, T0744-726385. Daily 0800-2130. Wine and good light meals just off piazza Garibaldi from the same management as **Il Pincio**. Tables outside are good for sunny days, and there are excellent spreads of local cured meats and cheeses.

Shopping

Orvieto *p88, map p88*
Books
Libreria dei Sette, corso Cavour 85,
T0763-344436. Mon-Fri 0900-1100, Sat-Sun
1000-2000. A good little bookshop with lots
of maps and guides.

Food and drink
Dai Fratelli, via del Duomo 11, T0763-
343965. Mon-Sat 0830-1330, 1700-2000,
closed Wed afternoon. A great selection of
pecorino as well as oozing gorgonzola and
jars of truffles. Despite its position in the
heart of the town, this delicatessen always
hums with locals as well as tourists.
Marco Ubaldini, piazza della Repubblica 29,
T3891-551449. Mon-Sat 0800-1330, 1700-
2000 (closed Wed afternoon). A tiny little
place packed high with delicious things,
from bread, cheese and cured meats to
delicious Rose del Deserto biscuits.
Ortofrutta, corso Cavour 236, T0763-
344716. An excellent little fruit and
veg shop selling fresh, local produce.
Also drinks and nuts.

Gifts
Michelangeli, via Gualverio Michelangeli 3,
T0763-342660, www.michelangeli.it.
Mon-Tue and Thu-Sat 0900-1300, 1600-
2000, Wed 0900-1300.
Una Pagina del Libro d'Oro, corso Cavour
307, T340-948 9628, info@librodoro.net.
A toy shop with a fine line in mechanical
wooden toys and 'paper animation' –
interesting things you can make that move.
A wander around the streets of Orvieto
will reveal wooden friezes and 'urban
furniture', on walls, on street corners and in
restaurants. Via Michelangeli has a particular
concentration, and the homonymous shops
of this 200-year-old Orvietan furniture
makers are also here, though these days
they have branched out into toys, puppets
and rocking horses, all with a charming
Orvietan style.

Homeware
Menabò, vicolo del Popolo 12/14, T0763-
393900. Mon-Sat 0930-1400, 1600-2100.
A great collection of Scandinavian, Italian
and international design items, with a good
line in kitchen gadgets, lights, stationery,
cutlery and colourful crockery.

Todi *p93*
Marco Cionco Antiquario, via Ciufelli 7,
no phone. Daily 1000-1300, 1530-1900.
An enormous selection of brass and
other metal antiques, from bells and
door knockers to lamps and corkscrews.

What to do

Orvieto *p88, map p88*
Cycling
Eurobici, via Angelo Costanzi 24, Orvieto
Scalo, T393-992 4469. If you fancy cycling
around the Route Rupe in Orvieto, or further
afield, **Eurobici** has bikes for rent.

Photography
Camera Etrusca, corso Cavour 273, Orvieto,
T0763-562005, www.cameraetrusca.com.
1-day courses from €200 per person,
residential courses from €699 for 4 days,
€1217 per week. Patrick Nicholas, a British
photographer, has lived in Italy for 27 years
and now has a gallery in Orvieto (daily
in summer, 0900-2000), where he does a
good trade in fine art Italian landscapes
and photographic nudes in the styles of
old masterpieces. He also runs guided
photographic trips and photo workshops
in the surrounding area. Residential courses
for small groups over 4 days or a week
include food, accommodation and, if need
be, kit. It's also possible to do 1-day trips.
Courses focus on landscapes in southwest
Umbria and parts of neighbouring Lazio
and Tuscany – the so-called *civiltà del tufo*.
His years of experience in the area mean
Patrick knows the best places to go for
great shots, and his technical know-how is
put to good use too. Courses can include

tuition in Adobe Photoshop and printing, and attendees are usually a good mix of experts and complete beginners.

Todi *p93*
Language courses
La Lingua la Vita, via Mazzini 18, Todi, T075-894 8364, www.lalingualavita.com. Courses of Italian lessons, from a week in length, start at €375 per person, including a double room.

❶ Directory

Orvieto *p88, map p88*
Hospital Ospedale Orvieto, via Sette Martiri 7, T0763-307366.

Pharmacy Farmacia del Moro, corso Cavour 89, T0763-344100, www.farmaciadelmoro.it.

Todi *p93*
Hospital viale di San Filippo, at the southeast corner of town.
Pharmacy Farmacia Ferdinandi Pirrami, piazza del Popolo 46, T075-894 2320.

Narni *p96*
Hospital via dei Cappuccini Nuovi 3, T0744-7401. **Pharmacy** Farmacia Pallotta, piazza Garibaldi 20/22, T0744-715267.

Contents

Background

History

Umbri, Etruscans and Picenes

Disproving the common belief that Italian culture started with the Romans, Umbria and Marche are rich sources of some sophisticated pre-Roman remains. The first populations probably migrated to central Italy from eastern and central Europe around 1500 BC, initially to the fertile plains around Perugia, then increasingly into the hills.

Earliest inhabitants

Little is known about the Umbri, the first sophisticated, organized civilization in the region. Pliny the Elder, writing in the first century AD, called them the oldest people in Italy, and their lands probably stretched to cover much of modern-day Tuscany and Marche as well as Umbria. There was a distinct and strict Umbrian social structure, probably based on military rank. The Iguvine or Eugubian Tablets, bronze plates discovered by a farmer near Gubbio in the 15th century, are engraved with Umbrian inscriptions that tell of religious rituals including sacrifices.

Etruscan culture

As the Etruscans spread from the northwest, the Umbri were pushed east, so that by around 700 BC the River Tiber was the dividing line between the two cultures, and the Etruscans controlled previously Umbrian towns such as Perugia and Orvieto. They traded extensively with the ancient Greeks, to the extent that around three-quarters of all Ancient Greek pottery discovered to date has been found in Italy.

Etruscan civilization was highly developed, of unknown origins, and with a mysterious non-Indo-European language. Modern genetic experiments on people living in the region suggest their Etruscan ancestors may have come from the Eastern Mediterranean. They seem to have been a loosely affiliated society, without a centralized power base. No history written by the Etruscans exists, though there are plenty of funerary inscriptions. The Etruscan tombs outside the walls of Orvieto are a rich source of information. There are also Etruscan tombs outside Perugia, and many sarcophagi in its archaeological museum. These carved stone coffins often portray the deceased reclining on the lid.

In comparison with ancient Greece, women seem to have been given more prominence in Etruscan society, with tombs possibly suggesting a matriarchal line of descent. Etruscan women, unlike Greek women, attended banquets, and some Etruscan carvings show affection between couples, which is usually absent from Greek depictions.

There is debate about the extent to which the Etruscans influenced the Romans – certainly much of Etruscan architectural style was adapted by the Romans, and some go as far as to suggest that the name Rome itself may be Etruscan. Ancient Etruscan walls and city gates can be seen in Orvieto and Perugia, where Emperor Augustus later added his stamp to one of the Etruscan gates.

The Picenes are the most obscure of the region's ancient peoples. A warlike bunch, they inhabited a small strip of present-day Marche, giving their name to the town of Ascoli Piceno. Many were buried in full battle garb, with swords (imported from the Balkans) and spears.

In 309 BC Perugia was defeated in battle against the Roman army and gradually, over the next 150 years, the entire Etruscan, Umbrian and Picene region fell under the control of Rome.

The Roman Empire

A power struggle followed the murder of Julius Caesar in 44 BC. Caesar's great-nephew Octavian forced Mark Antony's brother Lucius Antonius out of Rome; when he took refuge in Perugia, Octavian (now Emperor Augustus) destroyed the city, and with it the last remnants of Umbrian independence. The *Arco Etrusco* (Etruscan Arch) still bears the inscription that the emperor had placed on it – 'Augusta Perusia' – renaming the city after himself and stamping his authority on the region.

By this time Rome was already the dominant force in the whole region. Historians disagree about the exact level of the Etruscans' influence on the early Roman Empire: some believe that they may have had an important part to play in the founding of Rome itself. Once the two powers were competing for control of the region, however, the loose structure of Etruscan government was no match for the centralized power of Rome.

Roman settlements

The important via Flaminia, which connected Rome with the Adriatic at Fano, had a major influence on the region for many centuries. A part of the road, paved with stones on which Roman cartwheel grooves are still visible, can be seen at Carsulae, where it passes through the *Arco di Traiano* (Trajan's Arch), and much of the original Roman route is still used, including, at the Gola del Furlo, a tunnel through the rock constructed by Vespasian in AD 77.

As trade flowed through the region, Roman towns grew up, and earlier Umbrian towns expanded. Umbria became increasingly prosperous and strategically important. Romans took their holidays in Umbria, and emperors partied at the Fonti del Clitunno. Roman towns such as Interamna Nahars (Terni), Spoletium (Spoleto), Fulginium (Foligno) and Perusia (Perugia) thrived; historians described Narnia (Narni) in such glowing terms that CS Lewis later borrowed its name for his heavenly fictional world.

Roman Carsulae, in the hills north of Narni, grew up almost entirely because of its position on the road, and became a staging post complete with a theatre and amphitheatre complex, temples and a large triumphal arch. The via Flaminia was subsequently re-routed around the town, however, and an earthquake may have hastened its demise. Abandoned for centuries, it is now an important and idyllic archaeological site.

Life was not always simple for the Romans – they suffered one of their worst military defeats here in 217 BC, when the Carthaginian general Hannibal, having led his army, complete with elephants, over the Alps, lured a Roman army under Flaminius into an ambush and killed at least 15,000 soldiers.

Though the region's urban buildings are often of medieval origin, the layouts of many towns still follow the original Roman city plan, with a central piazza where the Roman forum once stood, and a main street that follows the route of the original east-west *decumanus maximus*. Towns such as Assisi were built over Roman foundations, and the front section of the original Roman temple still stands, now adapted into a church.

Almost everywhere you can find Roman carvings and columns reused by subsequent generations – the Tempietto sul Clitunno was thought to be a Roman temple, until it was realized that early Christians had reused parts of earlier Roman ruins to build their church. Many other churches in the region feature recycled Roman capitals and stones.

Eventually, the road that had given the region so much prominence also brought problems. As trade had travelled along the via Flaminia in the years of the Roman Empire, so Vandal and Visigoth invaders used it in subsequent centuries, and with the fall of the Western Empire the region was subjected to many major battles that ushered in a new, less ordered era.

The Dark Ages – early Christian and Gothic

As the Roman Empire declined and fell, into the post-Roman (Byzantine) era stormed the eastern Germanic Goths. Umbrian towns were destroyed as they found themselves caught in a strategically significant position between the two battling forces. With the disintegration of central government the region fragmented; the hills of Umbria, and the monastic traditions and practices they gave birth to, were to be essential to the survival of western Christianity.

The Lombards and the Duchy of Spoleto

The Goths ruled central Italy until the western Germanic Lombards, under King Alboin, successfully invaded in AD 568. The Lombards' Duchy of Spoleto covered most of modern-day Umbria, though the Byzantines retained a strip of central Italy from Rome to the Adriatic, including Narni and Perugia, cutting off the Duchy from the Lombard centre of power to the north but also giving it a degree of independence.

The Lombards had arrived with a fearsome reputation, but as they settled in the region they became less warlike, gave up their Arianism to embrace Catholicism, and contributed to the construction of abbeys. It was, eventually, a time of renewed stability and an era of importance for Spoleto, though little remains from the Lombard era – the Chiesa di San Pietro in Valle is an exception.

To the north, the Lombards overstretched themselves when they invaded Ravenna, upsetting the pope. In AD 754, Pope Stephen III consolidated the papacy's earthly power when he asked the Franks, under Pepin the Short and subsequently his son Charlemagne, to take up arms against the Lombards. Though the Duchy of Spoleto continued to exist as an entity until 1250, the balance of power had swung away from the Lombards, and the eighth century marked the beginning of a long and often uneasy relationship between the Franks and the pope; nominally partners in the Holy Roman Empire they were often bitterly opposed as they fought for economic control, not just of Italy but of the whole of Western Europe.

Birth of monasticism

While these power struggles were being played out, in the Umbrian hills, Benedict and Scholastica were born in Norcia in AD 480; they initiated a long spiritual tradition in the region that looked not to the grandiose papal style of Rome but to a more humble, meditative religion, which centuries later would culminate in the philosophy of St Francis.

At the same time the Benedictine influence gave to Western Europe a quiet – and at the time unheralded – tradition of learning, in the process preserving history and literature. Benedict founded 12 communities of monks and his 'Rule', the code by which the monks lived, was highly influential, though he never set out to found anything as far-reaching as a monastic order and was not canonized by the Roman Catholic Church until 1220. The Rule, actually a book of precepts summed up in the words *'pax, ora et labora'* ('peace, prayer and work'), was designed to set the foundations for religious communities living together. Widely adopted by monks and nuns ever since, it has been so successful that St Benedict is generally regarded as the founder of Western monasticism, his sister as the first nun.

The pope and the Holy Roman Empire

Struggles between the pope and the state have a long history in Italy, and Umbria and Marche have always been either involved in or affected by them.

In AD 776 the Duchy of Spoleto fell to Charlemagne and his Frankish army. Twenty years earlier, Charlemagne's father Pepin the Short, having captured Ravenna from the Lombards, had given it to the papacy in return for influence and titles. The Duchy of Spoleto was now also given to the pope, though Charlemagne retained the right to name its dukes. In AD 800, Pope Leo III crowned Charlemagne Holy Roman Emperor. It was a hugely significant moment for Western Europe, and central Italy was largely shaped by it for the next 1000 years.

In creating the notion of a Holy Roman Empire, Charlemagne built an entity to rival the power of the Byzantine Church to the east, merging Germanic power with historical memories of the Roman Empire and the spiritual authority of the papacy. At the same time the Papal States were born and the pope became involved in temporal power to an unprecedented extent, becoming a political and economic power as well as a spiritual one.

Guelphs and Ghibellines

The tensions created by this relationship between pope and emperor, and the vexed question of whether the Church gave authority to the emperor or vice versa, were played out at local levels, with powerful families and towns taking (and often switching) sides to suit their own ends.

By the 12th century, the faction on the side of the papacy had become known as the Guelphs; those in favour of the emperor were the Ghibellines. ('Guelf' was probably derived from the Bavarian dukes of the Welf, and 'Ghibelline' from the rival Hohenstaufens of Swabia, who used Waiblingen, the name of their castle, as a battle cry.) Associations were loose, however, and more often local than national. Guelphs often came from rich mercantile backgrounds and Ghibellines from agricultural estates. Born in Assisi in 1181, St Francis himself fought in this strife, taking part in battles against Perugia, where he was captured and imprisoned.

This background of centuries of local squabbles and bitter rivalries helped to create the Umbria and Marche landscape that still exists today, with fiercely protected castles and walled hill towns guarding local *comuni* (communes/municipalities), and strongly held local identities. Castles such as Gradara date from this period, and even important farms had their own watchtowers and defences, some of which still survive.

At times, larger forces washed over these local battles. When Frederick Hohenstaufen, known in Italy as Barbarossa, became emperor in 1152, he marched south, brutally overpowering and often destroying Umbrian cities that stood up to him, such as Spoleto. This imperial violence did not mean, however, that papal governors were received any more favourably – the rich, noble families of Perugia were particularly unhappy to be governed from Rome.

Pope Innocent III came to Umbria in 1216 to try to firm up his authority, but he died, probably poisoned, in Perugia. The regional antipathy towards the pope was political rather than religious, but a new-found religious enthusiasm was inspired by St Francis and had a profound influence on the region. And while it was often an anarchic and bloody period, in some ways the local competition and one-upmanship also paved the way for the architectural and artistic flowering of the Renaissance, as well as fostering the area's independent spirit.

The Renaissance and the end of self-government

The first green shoots of the Renaissance began to appear early in the region, when the papacy was split between Avignon and Rome in the 14th century – the so-called Western Schism. With Europe's attention focused elsewhere, Umbria and Marche were left largely to their own devices, and the *comuni*, which already enjoyed a degree of independence, flourished. Many of the structures of 21st-century Umbria and Marche date from the 14th and 15th centuries, years when the *comuni* had enough power and economic strength to define their own destinies.

Papal domination

It would, however, be wrong to characterize the medieval period as a golden era for the region. Bitter infighting continued, and it was a time notable as much for its bloodiness as for its cultural blossoming. Foreign *condottieri*, or mercenaries, were hired to fight on behalf of local towns and cities, increasing the violence. The streets of Perugia are said to have flowed with the blood of the murdered. Then there was the Black Death, which killed more than half the population in 1348. There was no understanding that bubonic plague was passed on by fleas on rats, and the disease recurred many times after the main outbreak was over. And there were earthquakes too. Eventually, weakened by fighting between themselves, the towns and cities of the region all fell to the papacy, and long centuries of neglect followed.

La Guerra del Sale – the Salt War – is a good example of the different military and economic influences of the times. In 1540, Pope Paul III told the citizens of Perugia that thenceforth they would be forced to purchase only papal salt, at a price that was more than double what they were currently paying. The justification given was that the income was needed to support the papal troops. The people of Perugia were not impressed and, after the failure of negotiations, war broke out between the city and the papacy. The pope won, took away all Perugia's independence and built a huge castle, the Rocca Paolina, on top of the city quarter where the rich Baglioni family had previously lived. It is said, perhaps apocryphally, that the absence of salt in the region's traditional bread dates from this point.

Artistic and intellectual growth

Given the misery and violence of everyday life in late medieval times, the flourishing of the arts seems incongruous, but it was around this time that the Renaissance court of Federico da Montefeltro became a famous centre of artistic patronage. Pietro Vannucci, better known as Perugino, was born in Città della Pieve in 1446; 37 years later his most famous student, Raphael, was born – the son of an artist at the Urbino court.

It was also a period of wider intellectual flowering. The first copy of Dante's *Divine Comedy* was printed in Foligno, in southern Umbria, in 1472, by which time universities were already thriving in Perugia and Macerata. It may have felt like an era of change and hopefulness, but it wasn't to last.

Under the firm but distant thumb of papal rule the region largely stagnated – isolated, rural and forgotten – until unification.

The Risorgimento to the present day

The Salt War was the final struggle of years of discord between the *comuni* and the papacy. Nearly 200 years earlier Pope Innocent VI had employed Cardinal Albornoz to subdue the region, and many of the papal fortresses he had built still lord it over towns such as Assisi and Spoleto today.

After Perugia finally caved in to the power of the papacy, the region entered a slow decline, though some towns, such as Urbino and Città di Castello, did manage to retain some independence for a while. In many ways this mirrored the fate of Italy in general – after the Renaissance, the European cultural and political status of the whole peninsula began to ebb away to the north.

Between the 16th and 18th centuries Umbria and Marche became something of a backwater. Depopulated and riven by banditry – in the late 16th century the papacy executed over 1000 bandits a year – the area languished as a largely unloved and isolated source of papal taxation. At the end of the 18th century Napoleon came and took control, then left again after a brief period of economic growth, having plundered the region's art and other treasures.

Unification and war

When, in 1859, Perugia rose up in favour of the Risorgimento (the movement to unify Italy), it can have come as no great surprise. When unification finally arrived, the inhabitants of the city celebrated by immediately demolishing the huge Rocca Paolina, the castle that had represented so many years of papal rule.

Despite the revival of the name 'Umbria' in 1870, life under the new Italian Republic was not much easier than before. Opened up to national competition after centuries of torpor, the Umbrian and Marche economies struggled to cope. And when, in the early 20th century, opportunities to escape presented themselves, thousands did so, emigrating to America in huge numbers. Those left behind turned increasingly to socialism and communism in search of economic solutions, though their hopes of change were dashed under the regime of Mussolini, who left his profile built into the Marche rocks at the Gola del Furlo. In the Second World War Foligno was badly bombed by Allied forces, as was Terni, whose armaments factories made it a strategic target. Many towns were also left scarred when the German forces retreated, destroying infrastructure as they went.

Reinvention

In the second half of the 20th century, despite continued emigration, civic pride returned as power filtered down to the regions, and Umbria and Marche began to benefit from tourism and small-scale business. Transport links were improved, and cultural events – from revived medieval festivals to new seasons of jazz and opera – brought some zest to the area. Also important has been the renaissance of Umbrian food, which is increasingly exported to the rest of Italy and beyond.

The 1997 Umbrian earthquake, and the 2009 earthquake in neighbouring Abruzzo, were setbacks for a region increasingly reliant on tourism. For some years people stayed away, and there was also some disquiet over the way money was channelled into big projects and not into re-housing the homeless. Now, however, Most Marchigiani look to the future with some optimism: theirs is a region finally on the up.

Art and architecture

Though it is a region often defined by its verdant landscape, what makes Umbria and Marche so special is the way that humans have interacted with this landscape for the last 2500 years, leaving their mark in the forms of buildings, roads and farms. The continuity is remarkable – town walls built before the Roman era have been patched up now and again but still survive, and even where the original structures no longer stand, designs for (and often stones from) buildings erected by the Romans have been reused.

Art, too, has made its mark on the region: Raphael was born here, and some of the most important art ever painted adorns the Basilica of di San Francesco in Assisi. It is a land of religious art, of Perugino, Pinturricchio and the Crivelli brothers, but also of the beginnings of something else: the region's landscape makes some significant appearances, and some of its portraits, such as those of Federico da Montefeltro and his wife Battista Sforza, are instantly recognizable. It's also a region with – somewhat unusually for Italy – some excellent 20th-century art, especially the Burri Collection in Città di Castello and the sculpture and paintings of Spoleto, Marcerata and Ascoli Piceno.

Etruscan and Roman art

Despite the wide spread of the Umbri across the region, they left little of their building and art. The Etruscans, however, seemingly obsessed with death and rituals, left a large body of artefacts in tombs around Umbria, and Romans built upon their legacy.

Richly decorated pottery and carved stone sarcophagi tell us most of what we know of Etruscan civilization. The Museo Archeologico Nazionale in Orvieto has frescoes from two Etruscan tombs, with figures attending a funeral banquet, which show an elegance in Etruscan art that is often overlooked. The tombs themselves, just outside Orvieto, are solid, square, stone structures.

Etruscan pottery

Much of the pottery found in Etruscan tombs comes from Greece. In fact, so keen were the Etruscans on Greek pottery that a lot of it was made with this export market in mind, and more Ancient Greek pottery has been found in Italy than in Greece. In time, the Etruscans copied and developed the Greek styles. Gradually, figures and animals appeared, almost always in profile. Oriental patterns appeared around 700 BC, and the characteristic 'black-figure' pottery, with human figures against a red ground, followed in the same century. This style was subsequently reversed, so that red figures appear against a black background.

Bucchero ware is the black, usually polished, pottery most often associated with the Etruscans, and there are plenty of examples in museums around the region, especially in Orvieto and Perugia. The colour was achieved by firing the pots in an atmosphere of carbon monoxide instead of oxygen. The best pieces are from the seventh and sixth centuries BC, influenced at first by Phoenician and Cypriot designs and later by Greek pottery.

Roman advances

Etruscan towns were designed, rather than growing organically, and had two main axes: the north–south *cardo* and the east-west *decumanus*, dividing each town into four quarters. The form was later adopted by the Romans, who also developed other Etruscan features, such as barrelled arches, good roads and excellent drainage systems and sewers. Rome had the military might, however, and came to dominate the region, building towns around the important via Flaminia, the road that connected Rome with the Adriatic. The Romans' invention of concrete in the first century BC meant that, while they took up Etruscan forms, their buildings could be bigger and stronger; their use of marble also meant that their decorations and statues were finer, and lasted longer.

Though there are few, if any, intact Roman buildings in the region, there are plenty of ruins, and also many Roman elements that were reused in later buildings. The Tempietto sul Clitunno contains so many Roman elements that it was long considered to be a Roman structure; the entire front section of the Temple of Minerva in Assisi was retained when it became a church; and the Basilica di San Salvatore in Spoleto uses Roman columns, capitals and carvings in a comically haphazard fashion.

Medieval art and architecture

After the Romans, art and architecture suffered for centuries – medieval works were either forgotten, or were destroyed in the many battles, and little of that period survives today. From around AD 1000 to the start of the Renaissance the conflict continued, but despite the Guelph-Ghibelline chaos (see page 111), or in some cases because of it, towns began to grow and prosper.

Competition between rival towns, and between Church and State, led to unprecedented architectural and artistic one-upmanship. While the wealthier and more powerful Church built bigger churches and cathedrals, towns such as Gubbio tried to exert their independence by building bigger and more impressive town halls and public buildings. Increased private wealth amongst merchants also meant that grand homes were constructed.

Byzantine art

The Church employed artists to decorate its new buildings, initially in a largely Byzantine style, with front-on portraits of the Madonna and Child on patterned backgrounds of gold leaf. As the period wore on, these became more sophisticated, culminating in the extraordinary storytelling frescoes of Giotto and Cimabue in the Basilica di San Francesco in Assisi, a crucial stepping-stone in the path towards the Renaissance and a modern concept of art.

From Romanesque to Gothic

This was also a time of changing styles in architecture. The Romanesque style, so-called because it used many of the round forms of ancient Roman architecture, can be seen in some of the region's oldest churches, such as at San Pietro in Valle and Sant'Eufemia in Spoleto both largely constructed in the 12th century. Buildings of this type combine sturdy walls with round arches, barrel vaults and large towers. Their symmetrical layouts are generally simple and their windows small.

Gothic style, which originated in France, was long regarded as inferior in central Italy – indeed the Italians coined the description 'Gothic' as an insult, because they equated the style with something barbaric. Nevertheless, it became increasingly influential, with its more complex ribbed vaulting, flying buttresses, pointed arches and high, light, stained-glass windows. The upper church in the Basilica di San Francesco is a good example of Umbrian Gothic at its best.

As Umbria and Marche came under papal control, political influence and power drained away; many towns in the region stagnated after the 15th century, retaining their medieval buildings and traditions. Wander around the centres of Umbrian hill towns such as Gubbio, Perugia or Assisi, and you might feel that in 500 years nothing much has changed.

The Renaissance

After the often flat, decorative, Byzantineinfluenced religious art of the medieval period, the artistic flowering of the Renaissance in the 15th century was a dramatic change. Influenced by the work of Giotto and a rediscovery of the forms and shapes understood in ancient Roman times, artists started painting three-dimensional space, light and shadow, rendering architectural perspective and including landscape and domestic detail. Though most art remained nominally religious, contemporary faces and emotions appeared in works that were often paid for by rich families. This patronage in turn created a cult of personality, and painters – who had previously been largely anonymous – became the celebrities of the age.

Umbria's great artists

Pietro Vannucci, known as Perugino, was born in Città della Pieve in 1446. His work marks the beginning, and arguably the apotheosis, of the so-called Umbrian school of Renaissance art. Perugino worked in the studio of Andrea del Verrocchio, alongside Leonardo da Vinci, and he may have also studied under Piero della Francesca. His greatest achievement was probably his tutoring of Raphael, though at his peak he also produced some great Renaissance art, before falling back into saccharine cliché later in his career. He was one of the most famous and successful painters of the time, and was called to Rome by the pope to paint the Sistine Chapel.

The Umbrian landscape, notably around the shores of Lake Trasimeno, features strongly in Perugino's art, and he clearly took his studies of perspective seriously. It is easy to see links between his painting and that of his pupil Raphael, but it is also possible to see how Raphael improved on what he had learnt.

Pinturicchio was a contemporary (and assistant) of Perugino, and is often overshadowed by him, sometimes rather unfairly. Though he was not an innovator like Perugino, Pinturicchio's decorative paintings exhibit a detached, careful draughtsmanship that has aged well and often appears quite contemporary next to Perugino's sentimentality. Born Bernardino di Betto in Perugia in 1454, Pinturicchio worked with Perugino on frescoes in the Sistine Chapel and later decorated rooms in the Vatican Library. His finely observed plants and landscapes mark him out as an artist with a very keen eye, and many of his paintings are embellished with fascinating minutiae.

Raffaello Sanzio (known in English as Raphael) was born in Urbino in 1483. His father Giovanni Santi was also an accomplished painter and poet, and was court artist to Federico da Montefeltro. Raphael was orphaned at the age of 11, but by then he had already worked with his father, and as a teenager he showed precocious talent. There is debate about when he worked as an assistant, and perhaps as an apprentice, to Perugino in Perugia, but by 1501 he was already described as a fully trained master. The depiction of Daniel in one of Perugino's sumptuous paintings in the Collegio del Cambio is probably a portrait of Raphael, and his own first documented fresco is also in Perugia, in the Cappella di San Severo.

Renaissance architecture

Though the region's great architecture is mainly medieval, there are some notable Renaissance buildings too, such as La Fortezza in San Leo and the Palazzo Ducale in Urbino.

Many medieval buildings, such as the Cattedrale di Santa Maria Assunta in Spoleto were given Renaissance additions.

Post-Renaissance

Under papal rule, the region's art and architecture largely stagnated for centuries. This lack of development has left many artistic treasures unspoilt, but it has also stunted artistic life. A 20th-century rebirth of sorts centred around Alberto Burri in Città di Castello. His abstract sculptures, full of pain and suffering, were a response to the violence of the period. His legacy has left sculpture as one of the region's foremost artistic outlets – Arnaldo Pomodoro's sculpture park and museum at Castello di Pietrarubbia in Marche is a fine example.

Burri's use of post-industrial space in the tobacco-drying sheds of Città di Castello is also one of the region's best examples of contemporary architecture. A drive through the ugly suburbs of Perugia or Ancona provides graphic evidence that interesting architecture of modern times is concentrated on reusing existing structures rather than on building beautiful new ones.

Contents

Footnotes

Language

In hotels and bigger restaurants, you'll usually find English is spoken. The further you go from the tourist centres, however, the more trouble you may have, unless you have at least a smattering of Italian.

Italians from the rest of the country often consider modern-day Marchigiani to speak with a rather slow, rural Italian, and though such attitudes are exaggerated, you may be able to detect a country lilt to some spoken language in the region. That said, it's seldom hard to understand.

Marchigiano dialect still exists, especially in rural areas, and sometimes in the names of traditional local dishes.

Vowels

a	like 'a' in cat		**i**	like 'i' in sip (except after c or g, see below)
e	like 'e' in vet, or slightly more open, like the 'ai' in air (except after c or g, see consonants below)		**o**	like 'o' in fox
			u	like 'ou' in soup

Consonants

Generally consonants sound the same as in English, though 'e' and 'i' after 'c' or 'g' make them soft (a 'ch' or a 'j' sound) and are silent themselves, whereas 'h' makes them hard (a 'k' or 'g' sound), the opposite to English. So ciao is pronounced 'chaow', but chiesa (church) is pronounced 'kee-ay-sa'.

The combination 'gli' is pronounced like the 'lli' in million, and 'gn' like 'ny' in Tanya.

Basics

thank you	*grazie*	goodnight	*buonanotte*
hi/goodbye	*ciao* (informal)	goodbye	*arrivederci*
good day		please	*per favore*
(until after lunch/		I'm sorry	*mi dispiace*
mid-afternoon)	*buongiorno*	excuse me	*permesso*
good evening		yes	*sì*
(after lunch)	*buonasera*	no	*no*

Numbers

1	*uno*	17	*diciassette*
2	*due*	18	*diciotto*
3	*tre*	19	*diciannove*
4	*quattro*	20	*venti*
5	*cinque*	21	*ventuno*
6	*sei*	22	*ventidue*
7	*sette*	30	*trenta*
8	*otto*	40	*quaranta*
9	*nove*	50	*cinquanta*
10	*dieci*	60	*sessanta*
11	*undici*	70	*settanta*
12	*dodici*	80	*ottanta*
13	*tredici*	90	*novanta*
14	*quattordici*	100	*cento*
15	*quindici*	200	*due cento*
16	*sedici*	1000	*mille*

Gestures

Italians are famously theatrical and animated in dialogue and use a variety of gestures.

Side of left palm on side of right wrist as right wrist is flicked up Go away

Hunched shoulders and arms lifted with palms of hands outwards What am I supposed to do?

Thumb, index and middle finger of hand together, wrist upturned and shaking What are you doing/what's going on?

Both palms together and moved up and down in front of stomach Same as above

All fingers of hand squeezed together To signify a place is packed full of people

Front or side of hand to chin 'Nothing', as in 'I don't understand' or 'I've had enough'

Flicking back of right ear To signify someone is gay

Index finger in cheek To signify good food

Questions

how?	*come?*	where?	*dove?*
how much?	*quanto?*	why?	*perché?*
when?	*quando?*	what?	*che cosa?*

Problems

I don't understand	*non capisco*
I don't know	*non lo so*
I don't speak Italian	*non parlo italiano*
How do you say ... (in Italian)?	*come si dice ... (in italiano)?*
Is there anyone who speaks English?	*c'è qualcuno che parla inglese?*

Shopping

this one/that one	*questo/quello*
less	*meno*
more	*di più*
how much is it/are they?	*quanto costa/costano?*
can I have ...?	*posso avere ...?*

Travelling

one ticket for...	*un biglietto per...*
single	*solo andata*
return	*andata e ritorno*
does this go to Como?	*questo va a Como?*
airport	*aeroporto*
bus stop	*fermata*
train	*treno*
car	*macchina*
taxi	*tassi*

Hotels

a double/single room	*una camera doppia/singola*
a double bed	*un letto matrimoniale*
bathroom	*bagno*
Is there a view?	*c'è un bel panorama?*
can I see the room?	*posso vedere la camera?*
when is breakfast?	*a che ora è la colazione?*
can I have the key?	*posso avere la chiave?*

Restaurants

can I have the bill please?	*posso avere il conto per favore?*
is there a menu?	*c'è un menù?*
what do you recommend?	*che cosa mi consegna?*
what's this?	*cos'è questo?*
where's the toilet?	*dov'è il bagno?*

Time

morning	*mattina*
afternoon	*pomeriggio*
evening	*sera*
night	*notte*
soon	*presto/fra poco*
later	*più tardi*
what time is it?	*che ore sono?*
today/tomorrow/yesterday	*oggi/domani/ieri*

Days

Monday	*lunedi*
Tuesday	*martedi*
Wednesday	*mercoledi*
Thursday	*giovedi*
Friday	*venerdi*
Saturday	*sabato*
Sunday	*domenica*

Conversation

alright	*va bene*
right then	*allora*
who knows!	*bo!/chi sa*
good luck!	*in bocca al lupo!*
	(literally, 'in the mouth of the wolf')
one moment	*un attimo*
hello (when answering a phone)	*pronto* (literally, 'ready')
let's go!	*andiamo!*
enough/stop	*basta!*
give up!	*dai!*
I like ...	*mi piace ...*
how's it going?	*come va?*
(well, thanks)	*(bene, grazie)*
how are you?	*come sta/stai?* (polite/informal)

Menu reader

General

affumicato smoked
al sangue rare
alla griglia grilled
antipasto starter/appetizer
aperto/chiuso open/closed
arrosto roasted
ben cotto well done
bollito boiled
caldo hot
cameriere/cameriera waiter/waitress
conto the bill
contorni side dishes
coperto cover charge
coppa/cono cone/cup
cotto cooked
cottura media medium
crudo raw
degustazione tasting menu of several dishes
dolce dessert
fatto in casa home-made
forno a legna wood-fired oven
freddo cold
fresco fresh, uncooked
fritto fried
menu turistico tourist menu
piccante spicy
prenotazione reservation
primo first course
ripieno a stuffing or something that is stuffed
secondo second course

Drinks (*bevande*)

acqua naturale/gassata/frizzante
   still/sparkling water
aperitivo drinks taken before dinner,
   often served with free snacks
bicchiere glass
birra beer
birra alla spina draught beer
bottiglia bottle
caffè coffee (ie espresso)
caffè macchiato/ristretto espresso with a
   dash of foamed milk/strong
spremuta freshly squeezed fruit juice

succo juice
vino bianco/rosato/rosso white/rosé/red wine

Fruit (*frutta*) and vegetables (*legumi*)

agrumi citrus fruits
amarena sour cherry
arancia orange
carciofio globe artichoke
castagne chestnuts
cipolle onions
cocomero water melon
contorno side dish, usually grilled
   vegetables or oven-baked potatoes
fichi figs
finocchio fennel
fragole strawberries
friarelli strong flavoured leaves of the
   broccoli family eaten with sausages
frutta fresca fresh fruit
funghi mushroom
lamponi raspberries
melagrana pomegranate
melanzana eggplant/aubergine
melone light coloured melon
mele apples
noci/nocciole walnuts/hazelnuts
patate potatoes, which can be *arroste* (roast),
   fritte (fried), *novelle* (new), *pure' di* (mashed)
patatine fritte chips
peperoncino chilli pepper
peperone peppers
pesche peaches
piselli peas
pomodoro tomato
rucola rocket
scarola leafy green vegetable used in
   torta di scarola pie
sciurilli or *fiorilli* tempura courgette flowers
spinaci spinach
verdure vegetables
zucca pumpkin

Meat (*carne*)

affettati misti mixed cured meat
agnello lamb
bistecca beef steak

bresaola thinly sliced, air-cured beef from Valtellina
carpaccio finely sliced raw meat (usually beef)
cinghiale boar
coda alla vaccinara oxtail
coniglio rabbit
involtini thinly sliced meat, rolled and stuffed
manzo beef
pollo chicken
polpette meatballs
polpettone meat loaf
porchetta roasted whole suckling pig
prosciutto ham – *cotto* cooked, *crudo* cured
salsicce pork sausage
salumi cured meats, usually served mixed (*salumi misto*) on a wooden platter
speck a type of cured, smoked ham
spiedini meat pieces grilled on a skewer
stufato meat stew
trippa tripe
vitello veal

Fish (*pesce*) and seafood (*frutti di mare*)
acciughe anchovies
aragosta lobster
baccalà salt cod
bottarga mullet-roe
branzino sea bass
calamari squid
cozze mussels
frittura di mare/frittura di paranza small fish, squid and shellfish lightly covered with flour and fried
frutti di mare seafood
gamberi shrimps/prawns
grigliata mista di pesce mixed grilled fish
orata gilt-head/sea bream
ostriche oysters
pesce spada swordfish
polpo octopus
sarde, sardine sardines
seppia cuttlefish
sogliola sole
spigola bass
stoccafisso stockfish
tonno tuna
triglia red mullet
trota trout
vongole clams

Dessert (*dolce*)
cornetto sweet croissant
crema custard
dolce dessert
gelato ice cream
granita flavoured crushed ice
macedonia (di frutta) fruit cocktail dessert with white wine
panettone type of fruit bread eaten at Christmas
semifreddo a partially frozen dessert
sorbetto sorbet
tiramisù rich 'pick-me-up' dessert
torta cake
zabaglione whipped egg yolks flavoured with Marsala wine
zuppa inglese English-style trifle

Other
aceto balsamico balsamic vinegar, usually from Modena
arborio type of rice used to make risotto
burro butter
calzone pizza dough rolled with the chef's choice of filling and then baked
casatiello lard bread
fagioli white beans
formaggi misti mixed cheese plate
formaggio cheese
frittata omelette
insalata salad
insalata Caprese salad of tomatoes, mozzarella and basil
latte milk
lenticchie lentils
mandorla almond
miele honey
olio oil
polenta cornmeal
pane bread
pane-integrale brown bread
pinoli pine nuts
provola cheese, sometimes with a smoky flavour
ragù a meaty sauce or ragout
riso rice
salsa sauce
sugo sauce or gravy
zuppa soup

Index

Titles available in the Footprint *Focus* range

Latin America	UK RRP	US RRP
Bahia & Salvador	£7.99	$11.95
Brazilian Amazon	£7.99	$11.95
Brazilian Pantanal	£6.99	$9.95
Buenos Aires & Pampas	£7.99	$11.95
Cartagena & Caribbean Coast	£7.99	$11.95
Costa Rica	£8.99	$12.95
Cuzco, La Paz & Lake Titicaca	£8.99	$12.95
El Salvador	£5.99	$8.95
Guadalajara & Pacific Coast	£6.99	$9.95
Guatemala	£8.99	$12.95
Guyana, Guyane & Suriname	£5.99	$8.95
Havana	£6.99	$9.95
Honduras	£7.99	$11.95
Nicaragua	£7.99	$11.95
Northeast Argentina & Uruguay	£8.99	$12.95
Paraguay	£5.99	$8.95
Quito & Galápagos Islands	£7.99	$11.95
Recife & Northeast Brazil	£7.99	$11.95
Rio de Janeiro	£8.99	$12.95
São Paulo	£5.99	$8.95
Uruguay	£6.99	$9.95
Venezuela	£8.99	$12.95
Yucatán Peninsula	£6.99	$9.95

Asia	UK RRP	US RRP
Angkor Wat	£5.99	$8.95
Bali & Lombok	£8.99	$12.95
Chennai & Tamil Nadu	£8.99	$12.95
Chiang Mai & Northern Thailand	£7.99	$11.95
Goa	£6.99	$9.95
Gulf of Thailand	£8.99	$12.95
Hanoi & Northern Vietnam	£8.99	$12.95
Ho Chi Minh City & Mekong Delta	£7.99	$11.95
Java	£7.99	$11.95
Kerala	£7.99	$11.95
Kolkata & West Bengal	£5.99	$8.95
Mumbai & Gujarat	£8.99	$12.95

Africa & Middle East	UK RRP	US RRP
Beirut	£6.99	$9.95
Cairo & Nile Delta	£8.99	$12.95
Damascus	£5.99	$8.95
Durban & KwaZulu Natal	£8.99	$12.95
Fès & Northern Morocco	£8.99	$12.95
Jerusalem	£8.99	$12.95
Johannesburg & Kruger National Park	£7.99	$11.95
Kenya's Beaches	£8.99	$12.95
Kilimanjaro & Northern Tanzania	£8.99	$12.95
Luxor to Aswan	£8.99	$12.95
Nairobi & Rift Valley	£7.99	$11.95
Red Sea & Sinai	£7.99	$11.95
Zanzibar & Pemba	£7.99	$11.95

Europe	UK RRP	US RRP
Bilbao & Basque Region	£6.99	$9.95
Brittany West Coast	£7.99	$11.95
Cádiz & Costa de la Luz	£6.99	$9.95
Granada & Sierra Nevada	£6.99	$9.95
Languedoc: Carcassonne to Montpellier	£7.99	$11.95
Málaga	£5.99	$8.95
Marseille & Western Provence	£7.99	$11.95
Orkney & Shetland Islands	£5.99	$8.95
Santander & Picos de Europa	£7.99	$11.95
Sardinia: Alghero & the North	£7.99	$11.95
Sardinia: Cagliari & the South	£7.99	$11.95
Seville	£5.99	$8.95
Sicily: Palermo & the Northwest	£7.99	$11.95
Sicily: Catania & the Southeast	£7.99	$11.95
Siena & Southern Tuscany	£7.99	$11.95
Sorrento, Capri & Amalfi Coast	£6.99	$9.95
Skye & Outer Hebrides	£6.99	$9.95
Verona & Lake Garda	£7.99	$11.95

North America	UK RRP	US RRP
Vancouver & Rockies	£8.99	$12.95

Australasia	UK RRP	US RRP
Brisbane & Queensland	£8.99	$12.95
Perth	£7.99	$11.95

For the latest books, e-books and a wealth of travel information, visit us at:
www.footprinttravelguides.com.

 footprinttravelguides.com

 Join us on facebook for the latest travel news, product releases, offers and amazing competitions:
www.facebook.com/footprintbooks.